Love is in the Air

~ 100 ideas for your personal wedding story ~

SUSAN ARTUP

MARRIAGE CELEBRANT

A Ceremony by Design
...true to your relationship...

This is an IndieMosh book

brought to you by MoshPit Publishing
an imprint of Mosher's Business Support Pty Ltd

PO Box 147
Hazelbrook NSW 2779

indiemosh.com.au

Cataloguing-in-Publication entry is available from the National Library of Australia: http://catalogue.nla.gov.au/

Title:	Love is in the Air
Subtitle:	100 ideas for your personal wedding story
Author:	Artup, Susan (1952–)
ISBNs:	978-1-922261-02-1 (paperback)
	978-1-925814-76-7 (ebook – epub)
	978-1-925814-77-4 (ebook – mobi)
Subjects:	Family Relationships/Marriage and Long-Term Relationships; Family Relationships/Love and Romance

Cover design and layout by Ally Mosher at allymosher.com

Front cover photo © Geoff Beatty at stillphotography.com.au

Back cover photo © Jeff Davies, Photographer

Internal images from Adobe Stock.

To all the couples who have honoured me
with the opportunity to conduct their
wedding, and of course to my husband,
the late, great Peter Benson.

Disclaimer

I have made every effort to ensure that the information in this book was correct at the time of publication. However, the publisher and I accept no liability for any loss, damage or disruption incurred by the reader or any other person arising from any action taken or not taken based on the content of this book. I recommend you seek third party advice and consider all options prior to making any decision or taking any action in regard to the content of this book.

I believe that most of the material used here is in the public domain. I have searched for any copyright holders of material I have used that may not be in the public domain. Some items are simply in reasonably well known (but unattributable) usage. However if there has been an unintentional breach of copyright, I invite you to contact me.

Contents

Chapter 7 "Theme" Weddings

Chapter 8 Poetry about Marriage

Chapter 9 What is Love anyway?

Chapter 10 Your Vows

About the Author

Chapter 1
My Wedding Story

1
Till death do us part

Your wedding story really has to start with my wedding story.

Back in the day I was influenced by Germaine Greer's book *The Female Eunuch*, which confirmed my own reality that motherhood wasn't for me and almost talked me out of getting married. That is until I met the love of my life and thought:

Well … why not?

And that is just it – we thought why *not* get married – we didn't get married because we needed commitment, or approval, or security. We got married because we already had that, and there was no reason not to get married. I still think that if marriage will make a difference to your relationship or that you think it will be a seal to guard against insecurity or threat – then you should really be evaluating your relationship first.

A marriage ceremony provides the legal framework for the commitment of heart and mind that you have already made as a couple. Marriage is called the cornerstone of society for just reason, but we all know of many strong and enduring relationships which do not bear its label. People do say that the formal commitment consolidates their relationship, but so does the passage of time and shared experience. However, I am not trying to talk you out of getting married!

We were married by a civil celebrant soon after the

option of a secular wedding was introduced by Lionel Murphy in the '70s … so different from one another, we never had to "work at it", or fought, or spent a night apart if we were in the same city.

Abnormal? But wedded, childless bliss till death did us part.

I meant every word of those marriage vows, as I will when I recite them for you as part of your personal wedding story.

2
A shared life

We were married in Dad and Mum's apartment in Fairy Bower in a very low-key ceremony on a Monday, the day after a surf carnival at Narrabeen … we eloped I guess you could say from the town in which we were living to be married in "secret".

I do understand couples who come to see me wanting their wedding to be as quiet and unobtrusive as possible. I think it was because I didn't want this most private and intimate intent to be made public property. Would I do that again? Maybe, maybe not – I do know that in the excitement of the day that people just want to wish you well, after all.

In the following decade or so I didn't think about the institution of marriage at all; I didn't even go to many weddings until I was invited to the wedding of a friend. She was married by a very well-known Northern Beaches celebrant in the Botanic Gardens – that's when I thought, *I could do that*. I thought there was enough theatre in me to create a mini-production for people, to design ceremony with the right words, the right flow with readings and music bespoke to them – true to their purpose, a reflection of their relationship, true to their relationship. So I set up "A Ceremony by Design" and though it has evolved over two decades now, I have not changed what I wrote in my first ceremony:

"... marriage is a partnership not entered into

lightly: it is a union based on love, loyalty and trust. It is a friendship too, where tolerance and understanding will grow, where good humour and respect for each other's individuality will allow each to flourish and find fulfilment.

Married life is a shared life, which, generous and sincere, allows a richer future of lighter burdens and increased joy.

Commitment in marriage means caring for your partner's welfare as for your own, being willing to listen, and encouraging each other in individual challenges.

Where forgiveness and open communication play a part, marriage will stand up to all the stresses inevitable in life: it is an enduring bond – it does not change under pressure. It is constant and true, and knows no measures or conditions."

Ideally followed by Shakespeare's Sonnet 116.

3

The way we were

When I started out I knew I would succeed because I had youth on my side. Oh, the confidence! I wasn't going to be like the other stuffy old celebrants (which they weren't) – youth was going to be my "point of difference". Nowadays it is experience.

When he was in business my father's slogan was "Quality is Value". He was a bit more expensive than the other butchers – but he sourced his "country-killed beef" in Blayney, not Homebush – that was the difference – and of course the wonderful customer service he provided. So I adopted "There is no Quality like Experience" in my promotion for my 20th anniversary.

I hope I bring all the charms of my youth with it too, and the value inspired by my dad. When the celebrant program started in the '70s and when I was appointed in 1995, couples didn't question the value of the celebrant as they do now, they respected the role as the social responsibility it was. All that has changed, however, and celebrants are now wedding service providers like any other and have to demonstrate their value constantly.

The process of getting married has remained fundamentally the same – but there have been some important changes. These days you must give a minimum of one month's notice to your celebrant – for years it had to be "one month and one day"; finally you may present your passport as evidence of place and date of birth – you don't have to scramble around to locate your birth certificate anymore; you now must show your driver's licence/ID card; and you are advised to apply to Births, Deaths and Marriages for a copy of your official, registered Certificate of Marriage after the wedding to prove and protect your ID.

These days weddings can be registered instantly online with the paperwork attached. My first celebrant instructional manual was type-written! I couldn't type anyway – becoming a celebrant was my motivation for this: I had to create documents.

Because of celebrancy, I became computer-literate and had a website from the start, although it was stilted and boring.

In 1995 nobody really thought about marriage equality. The phrase hadn't even been coined. Ironically, the section of the Marriage Act defining marriage could be applied more laterally – there were exemptions to the wording, "words to that effect" could be substituted, although rarely were. Now we are celebrating the triumph of inclusion, the "man and woman" definition is obsolete; love is love, and marriage is marriage.

The "vows" remain prescriptive – there is one accepted legal version, although you can add your own vows as well.

4

True to your relationship

In April 2015 I celebrated 20 years as a marriage celebrant. Although all weddings are special, I reflected fondly on my first couples commemorating their 20th wedding anniversary, while looking forward to working with new couples on their wedding and contributing to it the knowledge and approaches that I had gathered over the years. Despite the changes in law within the marriage celebrant program and indeed in the profile of the celebrant profession, one thing remained unaltered: the commitment of two people to each other in love and respect. My role remains to provide as much choice as possible in the wording of a ceremony, so that the tone and style envisaged for the day is honoured; it is also my role to ensure that everything is said and heard and registered according to law.

Then in 2016 I came of age as a celebrant – 21 years since I received my authorisation to change lives. I appreciated it as a serious charge … not to be trivialised (even though my favourite part is still throwing on a frock and reading out the poems in my best voice). My first weddings made an impact on me when I realised how seriously couples took my role. Then I knew that I had to come down to earth and make sure what I delivered was not only perfect in terms of the legalities I was entrusted to carry out, but seamless and truly reflective of the way couples wanted their relationship represented in public. It took over a decade for me to add the line "… true to your relationship …" in my branding of "A Ceremony by Design".

You can talk at length about how you want to serve couples and what you will give them, but these few words say it all. I have them on everything.

5
Coming of age

How things have changed over the years! In early days celebrants were appointed based on the service provided in their local postcode – if there was a need, they would be appointed upon approval of the Attorney General. There was not the plethora of choice you find today, nor the over-servicing, the competition, the anguishing over choosing the "best" celebrant.

Celebrants didn't do a training course, but were chosen on merit on the basis of their application, experience and references. These days they must complete a competency-based course after which they apply to become celebrants.

At the same time, celebrancy became an enterprise. When I started it was viewed as a service to the community and the fee was regulated to $125 per wedding. It was a vocational thing, not a business thing. Now celebrants can charge what they like, add complementary services to attract customers, offer themed weddings, stage-management, sound and light: with care not to diminish the solemnity of the occasion, and of the end result – to publicly and respectfully create a union.

In the original civil marriage program, we were to advertise in the Yellow Pages – in the *book*! We had to, we had to declare our presence in the community. Now couples don't even know what the 'phone book is. Back then websites were barely thought of, and all enquiries were made by 'phone – no email! The abundance of online wedding directories just didn't exist. Instead, there were the local paper and seasonal glossy wedding magazines – things you could actually pick up and see yourself advertising in as a celebrant – your advertising remained consistent, not dependent on the vicissitudes of Google.

Chapter 2
According to Law in Australia

6
What a celebrant must do

To protect you and make sure your celebrant knows what he or she is doing, the Commonwealth Attorney General has devised a code of conduct for its agents, so a marriage celebrant must:

- maintain a high standard of service – basically be professional
- recognise how important marriage and marriage ceremonies are to the community
- be aware of the law in regard to marriage and uphold it
- provide guidance to couples in choosing or creating a personal ceremony and make sure they know what will happen on the day
- make sure all legal documents are sighted and returned, keep an organised and secure office and make sure all documents are signed by all parties
- arrive at the ceremony 20 minutes before starting time and present the ceremony in an appropriate fashion
- accurately complete records and submit them to the registry, ask for feedback and advise of the grievance process
- be able to refer couples to family relationship services

As your celebrant I offer you much more than that –

elements which can't be prescribed in a code. It's the personal "je ne sais quoi" as well as the above that will make the difference on your wedding day and confirm your happiness as a couple. Rapport just happens and it is everything – this is part of an email I received from a couple after they booked me for their wedding:

> "You're an absolute gem and I love your energy. I am so happy you will be officiating at our marriage."

7

Essential paperwork

Sometimes couples are confused about the legalities surrounding the certification of marriage. First of all, you don't have to get a Marriage Licence in Australia. In its place, we have the Notice of Intended Marriage which is lodged, witnessed and held by the celebrant until after the marriage. This is the first thing you have to do in the legal process of getting married. It must be done at least a month before your wedding and not more than 18 months before.

On the Notice the celebrant has to note down the number on your driver's licence or ID card, the number on your passport or birth certificate and if you have been married previously the numbers of final divorce documents or death certificates. All these must be originals, not even certified copies. After the wedding the Notice of Intended Marriage is sent off to Births, Deaths and Marriages with your official Certificate of Marriage. This is the certificate that counts if you want to change your name, or use a "married" name – this is proof of ID. You don't have to apply to change your name after marriage. You can commence to use a different surname straightaway but to prove your ID, that you are the same person using more than one name, you will need to apply to get a copy of this Certificate of Marriage from BDM after it has been registered.

On the wedding day you sign three legal documents:

an elegant, commemorative certificate which you keep (proof and souvenir of your marriage), the register (the celebrant's copy) and an ordinary-looking form, which is your Certificate of Marriage that goes to BDM. BDM processes this and when you apply for it they send you back an official copy – proof of your marital names and ID which you can then present when changing the name on documents at the bank, Roads and Maritime Services, passport office etc. To apply for this certificate you can download a form from the BDM website or I can provide you with one.

8

The first thing you need to do

The Notice of Intended Marriage is usually and ideally provided, filled out and witnessed by me. Sometimes though it may be difficult to make an appointment to see me if you live somewhere distant and time is running out – in this case you can download the form from the website of Births, Deaths and Marriages in NSW at www.bdm.nsw.gov.au

You would then need to have it witnessed by a Justice of the Peace or any of the other authorities listed on the back of the form. After this you can either scan it and email it to me or post the original so that I have it a month before the wedding. Then your wedding Notice is "lodged". However, bear in mind that I MUST be given the original before I am permitted to proceed with the wedding.

At the time of filling out this form you also need to show me your original birth certificates or your passports so I can verify your ID and age. I must also see your driver's licence or ID card. If you've been married before I also need to see your *final* divorce papers (with the words "final", "absolute" or "termination" on them). If you can't place any of these documents in time for filling out the Notice of Intended Marriage, you can show them to me later, as long as I see them before the wedding date. Again, without them, I am unable to proceed by law.

To get an original copy of your birth certificate, you will go to BDM. To get an original copy of your divorce papers, you will need to go to the Family Court in which your divorce was granted. As there is quite a variation in these documents, it is important that I see them as soon as possible in case you have to do further searches.

9

Getting married in a hurry

What can you do if you need to get married and you don't have the luxury of giving a month's notice?

Although by law you must give this notice, it is possible to hold a wedding in a shorter time: this is called a "Shortening". A Shortening is not to be taken for granted, but can be applied for from a "Prescribed Authority" or magistrate at a local courthouse. Circumstances which may call for a Shortening are these:

- employment or travel commitments
- wedding or celebration arrangements
- religious considerations
- medical reasons
- legal proceedings
- error in lodging the Notice

The only reason I have ever been asked to conduct a wedding with a Shortening has been compassionate – the doubt that a party to the marriage or a family member may not live long enough for the prescribed period of notice.

If you need to be married in a short time frame, you should prepare your case and take a completed Notice of Intended Marriage (the only time this form can leave the celebrant's hands) from me so permission can be recorded on it. In addition I will give you a letter on my letterhead saying I have received your Notice and that I am willing and able to conduct your wedding pending the granting of your Shortening. Then you should return to the celebrant with the Notice and hopefully your wedding can go ahead as you wish.

10
Choosing your ceremony

At our first meeting I will give you a ceremony information pack based on more than a thousand ceremonies from over 20 years. There are not a thousand to choose from but a number of "standard" ceremony proformas and a number of variations on these. It's been a privilege to build up this collection based on the generous sharing of ideas of the couples I've met: special symbols, rituals and readings from many cultures and spiritual outlooks.

After you lodge your Notice of Intended Marriage with me I will give you an information leaflet called "Happily Ever Before and After" from the Department of Family and Community Affairs. I am obliged to give you this, as well as information about relationship education in the community. As a marriage celebrant I am not a relationship educator or counsellor and do not presume any such role – but the government sees it important that I should have access to this information for you.

I see my role as twofold: to make sure that your ceremony and its preparation incorporates all the elements and processes required by law – i.e. to pin you down; and to give you as many options as possible to make your ceremony individual and unique, "true to your relationship" – i.e. to give you freedom.

This is why I'll give you the ceremonies and readings

to choose from and even more importantly will be open and willing to listen to any ideas you have about how you'd like your ceremony to unfold – anything you've seen or heard and collected over the years can be woven into your ceremony – and remember, I am the facilitator, the official presence – I can be more in the background than you may think if you or a close friend or family member want to play a prominent role in the proceedings.

11

A ceremony formula

The ceremonies I give you to choose from or mix and match are just suggestions – you can ignore it all and start again with your own words and just use my ceremonies as a guide to what you want to include.

Incorporating the legal parts, a ceremony would have about nine steps, excluding readings. The steps follow a logical sequence, and the words from the Marriage Act must be near the beginning. However you can be creative and not only write your own content but play around with the sequence – you can be as theatrical as you please while maintaining an element of solemnity. My booklet gives you a lot of examples of how other couples have broken the mould. After all, you've chosen not to be married in a church – a civil ceremony is your licence to be different!

These are the nine steps:

1. The Introduction
2. The Marriage Act
3. The Giving Away
4. The Asking
5. The Vows
6. The Rings
7. The Declaration of Marriage
8. The Signing of the Register and two Certificates
9. The Presentation of the Newly Married Couple

Voilà!

12

Your homework

Your homework is due at our second meeting!

There are some things to bear in mind when designing your ceremony:

- The vows and ring presentation are usually repeated after the celebrant – i.e. it is not necessary to memorise them

- Before the vows are taken, the celebrant will say "I will now ask you to make your marriage vows. Please face each other and joining hands, and looking at each other, repeat after me …"

- Before the rings are exchanged the celebrant will say "Please take the ring and holding it over the ring finger of your betrothed's left hand, repeat after me: (your choice of words) … and slip the ring on her/his finger."

Designing your ceremony, choosing the promises that you intend to make to each other – this is the *foundation* of your marriage. Don't underestimate its value.

I'm supposed to give you information on marriage education – in my view working on your ceremony together is a wonderful exercise in relationship-strengthening.

One couple sent me a message about this:

"We found this harder to do than we expected.

I would find myself weeping ... This is not like me. I felt moved by the words, and we both find ourselves nervous. You can live together, but there is more to it when you decide to marry. A 'formality' has taken on a different meaning ... it will mark a new beginning."

At your second meeting with me we can run through the ceremony you have put together (or haven't – I can always do all of it for you) and talk about how you envisage the minutiae of the ceremony to unfold.

This time between meetings is the opportunity for you to mull over and bring into focus how you want to be on the day ... and what kind of mood you want for your family and friends.

13

On the day

There are no hard and fast rules as to how you should organise the official part of your wedding – the *civil* ceremony was conceived so that you, the couple, could design proceedings to reflect your individual style, beliefs, culture and personality. The ceremony you choose, or write, can be traditional or unconventional; ritualistic or simple.

Much will depend on the number of guests you have invited. If you are having a big wedding it is recommended to have ushers arrive half an hour before starting time to greet guests and direct them to the venue.

If you are arriving separately, one partner and attendants should be present at least fifteen minutes before the start and stand close to the celebrant so that the ceremony can begin as soon as the other partner arrives. This partner will arrive a few minutes before the proceedings with the person "presenting" or "giving away" (optional), and attendants. He or she then proceeds down the "aisle" on the left of this person, followed by or following attendants, to stand on the left of the waiting partner. You will stand flanked by your attendants (or with no attendants) in a kind of semi-circle. I usually stand off to the side – not in the middle, 'presiding' over you.

If you are arriving together, you and the wedding party – at least the two witnesses, should meet the celebrant away from the guests a few minutes before the ceremony, and then proceed to the location decided upon for the wedding. The celebrant will normally come forward first and invite the guests to come closer. It is usual that you will stand facing the guests.

The ceremony you have chosen will then begin. Afterwards you will recess down the "aisle" or just disperse with the wedding party so that everyone can come forward and congratulate you.

The ceremony takes 20 – 30 minutes, after which the celebrant makes a quiet exit.

Music can be incorporated into the ceremony as you wish – e.g. during the processional, the signing of the register and recessional.

Remember that these are only guidelines – essentially you can decide the seating, standing, timing arrangements – as long as the legal requirements are met.

14

Fashionably late

This is a delicate matter for me to write about … even though I haven't been kept waiting to begin a ceremony for years it is still relevant for me to talk about it: the "tradition" of running late to your wedding.

Keeping your family and friends standing out in the blazing sun or in the chill of a cold snap does not endear you to them, nor does it create a convivial mood. They have come to honour you and you need to think of them.

Being late is often caused by your service providers – hairdressers taking too long, photographers holding you up, wedding cars arriving late … but these people are professionals and you should confirm with them the time your ceremony is scheduled to start – then they can allocate the time they know they will need to get you to the church on time.

Being "fashionably late" could throw out your day and compromise your celebrations: caterers will be depending on a time to start the food service, photographers will see their light dissipating, you may even have to cut your reception short …

As your celebrant I'll be anxious that you should have a happy, momentous and hassle-free occasion – so I'll be there in good time to allay any nerves.

15
After the wedding

On the day of the wedding you will sign three documents.

You will also need two witnesses over the age of 18 to sign these. You will sign in the name you have been using, or the name on your birth certificate. The signature should be consistent on all the documents of marriage, including the Notice of Intended Marriage.

Once your commemorative certificate, my register and the official Certificate of Marriage are signed, we will stand up from the signing table and I will introduce you, in words that you have chosen, for the first time as a married couple.

I present you with or leave you with your commemorative certificate of marriage and then I depart. If I don't have a chance to say goodbye to you it is because you will be surrounded by family and friends and it would be inappropriate for me to catch your attention and break into this melée of goodwill and congratulating. It isn't about me anymore! So I will make a quiet departure, wishing you well nonetheless.

Then I have two weeks to send your official Certificate of Marriage and Notice to Births, Deaths and Marriages for registration, although you are legally and irreversibly married as soon as you have made the legal commitment to each other.

In reality, I register your wedding online instantly and

send your documents electronically when I return to my office, where I securely keep my wedding register.

So, three pieces of evidence of your marriage will be signed by five people.

It is the official Certificate of Marriage that I send to the registrar that is evidence of your marriage and proof of your ID. You are advised to apply for this from BDM on the form that I give you or which you can download from the BDM website. Then if you begin to use a different surname, or two surnames, you have proof that you are that person. When people change their name on passports, licences and bank accounts, this is the document they will be asked for as proof of ID.

In addition to obtaining this certificate, couples from some overseas countries will need to take it to the Department of Foreign Affairs and Trade to have an apostille stamped on the back. They should find out what is required from their own governments before getting married in Australia in order to make the process smoother.

Chapter 3
Equality, Commitments and Reaffirmations

16
The search for love

I was a straight, white, protestant, theatrical girl from the north shore when I went to university in the early 1970s and made my first gay friends. It was not my priority to find a husband and have children so I found I had much in common with these fresh, funny gorgeous camp men. In those days, it wasn't theirs either. These men appealed to me because of their difference, their rising above the norm, and because we related to one another so well. Because of them, a whole world of culture and sophistication opened up to me, and an upfront and uncomplicated attitude to sex. Their attitude to love, though, and relationships, was just as tortured, and driven, and relentless. They wanted what everyone wanted – the opportunity to find a partner and commit, one day or another. In 1975 "marriage" was not named as an agenda item for the gay community. In fact in those days, depending on where you went and what you did, it was downright dangerous to be "out". However, my friends and I just had fun and I was naïve about the discrimination and prejudice that they must have been dodging on a regular basis. Homosexuality was no big deal to me … finally your friends are just your friends and their makeup and background are just part of the fabric of friendship.

A great deal of our fun was in the pursuit of attractive men. With every failure, constant craving kept us looking for "love", relentlessly searching for a partner, for "the one". In mature years I ponder this – why so many of us are addicted to making the "wrong" choices in love. We humans are fundamentally driven to be coupled, even if we don't want to create a family. Society and history have programmed us to believe that to be complete we need another, an equal and opposite, a reflection of ourselves, someone to witness our lives.

However, according to Greek mythology we were once complete in ourselves. In the one body we were any combination of male/female, male/male, or female/female. We were autonomous, independent and had no need to search for "wholeness". Our self-satisfaction and self-importance grew and brought the wrath of the gods, and as punishment we were split into two. Two halves of a whole scattered over the earth. And so the search began: our drive to find our other half, the missing piece that would make us complete again. Repeatedly we try, we have near misses, we are often wide of the mark, sometimes we settle for less than a perfect fit, and sometimes we can be lucky.

This is the happy coincidence that we celebrate at a wedding.

17

A piece of paper

There was something of a residue of 1960's free love in the mid-seventies: marriage was regarded in some circles as a conventional option, foisted upon us by society's expectations. "Marriage is just a piece of paper", we said — one which we did not need to prove our commitment or the seriousness of our relationship.

Feminism, too, convinced women that they should not be defined by their marital status. Gay men and enlightened women had that in common: absence of the expectation to enter into the legal bond of marriage. We were free of it.

In the new millennium things are quite different: to be free to meet the expectation is what everybody wants. Now Australians have called for marriage equality, the freedom for all to enter into the legal bond of marriage. Everybody now has the right to the piece of paper.

Commitment ceremonies were performed by civil celebrants, but this way is simply not enough anymore without the choice of the other, widely recognised rite.

However, commitment ceremonies are still an option if you don't want to be conventional but you still want to declare your union. This may be for many, individual, personal reasons. When celebrants undergo their annual mandatory professional development they are reminded of what constitutes marriage according to Australian law. It is an offence for a celebrant to give the impression that a commitment ceremony is a marriage ceremony. A celebrant is not supposed to give the impression that a legal marriage is taking place. So the words "husband", "wife", "spouse" even "marriage" should be avoided and somewhere it must be clearly stated that what is happening is not a marriage but a commitment ceremony.

18
What's in a word?

Marriage. The word has become so charged. It is locked in as the legal definition of commitment in a relationship. By extension, the word is bandied around more liberally: it has come to mean a blending, a natural joining, a dovetailing – minds can "marry", ideas can "marry", hearts can still "marry" – such "marriage" just happens.

Where the words describing marriage come from is interesting and adds to an understanding of the definition we hold today.

This word "marriage" comes from the Latin "maritare" meaning "to provide a husband or wife".

"Husband" comes from Old Norse, "husbondi" originally meaning "a householder", then evolving to refer to a manager of resources, including financial resources.

That is what " husbandry" in agriculture still means.

"Wife" comes from the Old English word "wif", meaning "woman" and surviving in "midwife" and "housewife". The word is related to the German word "Weib" which still means a woman of unrefined status – surviving in "fishwife". The German word "Frau" elevates a woman to marital status and is what is used today.

"Spouse" is from the Latin "sponsus" (groom) and sponsa (bride). These words come from "spondere" meaning to "solemnly promise" and to "bind oneself".

Our word "sponsor" also comes from this with its meaning of providing a guarantee, an expression of faith, assurance and confidence. Your spouse is the witness to your life, your support and your safety net.

As such, spouses come together in a union. "Union" comes from the Sanskrit, "jugum", a kind of yoke, a support structure which joins two parts. We see this today in "jugular" and "conjugate". This yoke joins two in sharing the ups and downs of life. This union is marked by a wedding. A wedding leads to a marriage.

The word "wedding" comes from Old Norse – Danish "vedde" and has evolved to modern German "Wette" which means "a bet" and extends to "a pledge" or "a vow". Orignally, a wedding was a business contact and marriage was the transaction that followed.

Another charming name for a wedding was the Old English,"bridalope" – the running of a bride to her new home. Our modern word "elope" – running away to be married, comes straight from this.

Words are not just words – their etymology explains many social attitudes and usage changes along with these.

Perhaps, from 2018, we need some completely new words.

19
Changes in legislation

On the 9th of December 2017 long-awaited and fought-for changes were applied to the Marriage Act. The Attorney General sent out these words to marriage celebrants:

> "... the right to marry in Australia will no longer be determined by sex or gender".

Accordingly, the compulsory wording defining marriage in a wedding ceremony was changed to "Marriage, according to law in Australia, is the union of two people to the exclusion of all others, voluntarily entered into for life."

In addition, couples could choose the way they wanted to be described irrespective of their gender. You can now be two wives, two husbands, husband and wife, wife and husband, spouses or married partners. The legal vows were changed to reflect this.

Far from the changes in law, the decision of the people late in 2017 was a triumph for inclusiveness and social acceptance. The result on December 9th was a very happy, historical day.

As were the many ceremonies between same-sex couples I have conducted since January 9th, the first day marriages lodged on December 9th could go ahead.

These ceremonies have been defined by freshness and joy – every one has been unique. Wedding conventions have been eschewed, adapted or celebrated. Venues have been pubs, restaurants, clubs, chapels, gardens and homes. Ceremonies have been colourful and funny, soft and reflective, high profile or low-key. It's a privilege to announce any couple's transition into marriage, but gay ceremonies have left me overwhelmed.

With same-sex marriage we've entered a new era of creativity and gratitude for the opportunity to partner in love, security and permanence.

Love rules!

20
Commitment ceremonies

Commitment ceremonies are for everyone. They are an option for anyone not in a position to fulfil the legal requirements of marriage. This may be because the mandatory notice hasn't been given, or dissolution documents haven't been found. A commitment ceremony is a choice; not dependent on law to hold it together, such a union can arguably be stronger than marriage.

There is nothing to stop you having two ceremonies, as long as only one is the legal version. One couple had been married already in a smaller ceremony with restrictions of location and time and wanted the major celebration to be a commitment ceremony. Another wanted a commitment ceremony followed by the legal marriage.

Yet another couple had lived together for decades, had children, and a home – he repeatedly asked her to marry him, but for whatever reason, it was never the right time. What she really wanted to do was to surprise him on his birthday with a wedding ceremony. Even though only one of the parties to marriage needs to sign off on the Notice of Intent a month before the ceremony, and the other can sign right up to the wedding, this really is not acceptable by law. The bride knew this and suggested we do a commitment ceremony, which was to be the bigger celebration of their union, when all their family and best friends were gathered. We had to omit any part that suggested that this was the marriage: in fact it had to be stated that it wasn't. No legal documents were signed but the ceremony came from the heart and included beautiful sentiments and readings.

And the groom had his surprise when the bride dropped to one knee, proffered a wedding ring and popped the question. Of course he said yes!

In place of the marriage certificates we signed a commitment certificate and the Notice of Intended Marriage. It was official!

21
Reaffirmation ceremonies

These ceremonies are often called Renewal of Vows ceremonies and it is just a matter of personal taste which is applied – maybe Reaffirmation is appropriate if the ceremony comes shortly after the original wedding, and Renewal of Vows more aptly applies on a significant anniversary. In any case, like commitments, renewals and reaffirmations are not legal ceremonies and it is an offence to give the impression that they are. In law you can only be married once. Yet these ceremonies can have a very important historical place in the process of being married and in living in marriage. I have conducted some of these ceremonies shortly after the legal wedding has taken place – this may have been overseas with a different group of guests and the reaffirmation was a reflection of that ceremony minus the legal wording for the benefit of guests at home. Sometimes a couple has eloped already and has saved the party and some other form of ceremony until another time and location for family and friends. Sometimes this arrangement is for logistical reasons.

For more romantic reasons, however, is a second ceremony to celebrate an anniversary – this is where vows are "renewed" (as opposed to restated).

Vow Renewals can take place decades after the actual wedding and can be really moving – they can tell a story of a marriage, children reared, homes lived in, travels, careers and changes: and still love endures. The same or different vows can be taken (not of course the vows from the Marriage Act) and the ceremony can really reflect on what marriage is according to law – "to the exclusion of all others, voluntarily entered into for life."

This is an opportunity to create a truly original ceremony with readings and sentiments stored up over the years. The original witnesses to the marriage can be used – and it would be interesting to consider which of the original friends have stood the test of guest-list time!

Chapter 4
Your Wedding Space

22
In the beginning

I was appointed an authorised civil marriage celebrant in April of 1995 and can remember the excitement of my first booking. I got all dressed up in a wedding outfit and went over to visit the entire family of the bride, the groom in attendance too. The mother of the bride teared up when I read a romantic poem by way of exhibiting my talents. I think I must have been a bit stiff and business-like, but I still bump into members of that family and that is a warm and fuzzy thing.

My first actual wedding was on July 29th in a private home somewhere near Blacktown. Standing in a corner of the lounge room on this winter afternoon, the bride and groom looked at me so intently, looking to me to allow them this moment of passage. I will never forget the looks on their faces, giving *me* the privilege!

My second wedding was in the beautiful Everglades Gardens in Leura – a venue in which I have now done hundreds of weddings.

My third wedding was out at Camden Valley Inn in their chapel – I was so chuffed with myself I nearly forgot to sign the marriage certificate for the couple, and I left the audience on their feet throughout. I have come a long way … and those marriages are more than 20 years old now.

When I told my first couple afterwards that theirs was my first wedding, but I didn't want to tell them that *before* the ceremony, they said they would still have asked me *because* it was my first! How lovely people are.

23
Any time, any place

Nurragingy, Nepean Weir, The Nepean Belle,
Mulgoa Valley Receptions, Lewers Gallery,
Norman Lindsay's

One of the main things a civil ceremony had going for it in the '70s was the idea of choice – the couple's choice as opposed to the church's decision. Choice of location being the thing that allowed for the first time so much freedom for creativity and design. A Commonwealth authorised celebrant can marry a couple anywhere within Australia or its territorial waters. Unfortunately you couldn't fly me to Bali to do your ceremony.

Nowadays I do a lot of weddings in the Blue Mountains, the Hawkesbury and the Northern Beaches, but looking over my registers, I conducted my first ceremonies in private homes and gardens on the Western Plain – Nurragingy Reserve at Doonside is still an extraordinarily busy spot to be married, with a reception centre and various gazebos and garden areas from which to choose to celebrate your nuptials. Settlers at Mulgoa and Mamre Homestead at St Marys also provided unique, intimate wedding venues. Mulgoa Valley Receptions is the 21st century version of these – seemingly out in the country but easily accessible to Penrith. Another favourite was the Log Cabin until it burned to the ground a few years ago.

If you don't want to venture all the way up the mountains to be married but still want a natural setting, you need go no further than the banks of the Nepean – the Nepean Weir along from the rowing club is a very popular location – you would have to book it with Penrith Council, as you would any spot along the river, such as Tench Reserve on the other side of Victoria Bridge. Anywhere along the bank is lovely – but you can always leave it and tie the knot as you roll down the river on the Nepean Belle paddle steamer.

These venues show off the backdrop of the river as perfect for weddings: the river often more reliable than the mountains.

Along the Nepean river too you'll find the Lewers Gallery with its original house and lush garden. Galleries like this are ideal for smaller weddings – when I started to do ceremonies at Norman Lindsay's Gallery at Faulconbridge I was told that we even were doing the signing on Norman's own little escritoire and that we should be careful not to scratch it!

24
Mountain elegance

The Officers' Mess at Glenbrook, Leuralla,
Everglades, Lilianfels, Echoes

From time to time over the years I've been fortunate enough to conduct weddings in the RAAF base at Glenbrook – usually the general public can't get a look-in there. The views down to the city are stunning and the Officers' Mess is steeped in timeless elegance and tradition. But you have to work in Defence to use the facilities: yes, I am talking men (and women) in uniform. Actually I've conducted a lot of weddings of men in uniform – one a Canadian Mountie – his wife-to-be asked me if I'd mind his wearing the full regalia! Really? Did I *mind*???

Anyway then I moved up the mountains to venues in Leura: places like Leuralla with its stone amphitheatre on the edge of the valley and the Everglades Gardens so beautifully crafted around the historic Sorensen home … such an elegant venue with a choice of manicured lawns and garden areas. These places are really a world away, and so private for a wedding.

I've been conducting weddings steadily at Lilianfels in Katoomba for over 20 years: it is an amazing luxury property with the feel of a guesthouse, so personal is the attention of the staff – especially if you are celebrating your wedding there. The usual venue is the Oak Garden, a triangular shaped hedged English garden, again so private and stylish.

And then if you cross the road there is Echoes, a boutique hotel with a stunning valley view. I've conducted many weddings there too, where couples can book out the whole property with their accommodation and settle back to be wined and dined in its fabulous restaurant! So many options … but if you really want your own space, you might think about a private guest house …

25
A place like home

Avonleigh, Glenella, Little Company Retreat,
The Hideaway, Kubba Roonga, Balquhain, The Chalet,
Silvermere, Allview Escape

If you'd like to be married at home but can't bear the idea of getting the place – house and garden – ready for guests, the catering and the cleaning up, you might consider having your wedding in a guesthouse or a Bed and Breakfast. I've done some really lovely, personal and relaxed weddings in properties like this. The mountains are scattered with them. Depending how tourism describes them these properties invite you to make yourself at home with every luxury appointment at your fingertips. Sometimes the owners are in residence and hang around in the background, but often couples I have married have hired a country cottage, complete with fireplace in autumn or newly-blooming garden in spring, and move in for the weekend. Some of these weddings have been very small and intimate – just the couple and their witnesses, and they have self-catered and settled in for a weekend getaway.

In places with a number of bedrooms, couples have organised a big weekend party for family and friends, brought in caterers and even a band. In any case they had the run of the venue with kitchen, lounge areas, bathrooms, outdoor terraces … every comfort of home but with no preparation or cleaning up! Just the joy of breezing in as two people and out as a married couple with all their favourite people in attendance. Places such as Avonleigh, The Glenella, The Little Company Retreat, The Hideaway, Kubba Roonga, Balquhain, The Chalet are all guesthouses in which I conducted weddings when I first started – and they are still going strong. Recently I've been impressed by the grace and charm of Silvermere at Wentworth Falls and the remoteness and breathtaking views of Allview Escape at Blackheath – both quite different from each other, depending on the number and taste of your guests.

26
Evans Lookout, Blackheath

You might like this little story if you are thinking of having a Blue Mountains wedding:

The weather this early summer has been unseasonably cold, yet for today it was perfect. Not in fact too cold, it contributed to the perfect stillness of the setting at Evans Lookout. Not a leaf moving, not a ray of sunlight to impose on the majesty of the cliffs and the bush. Just a collective awareness of nature and man, a reverence, quiet and pervasive. Around 50 guests of all ages assembled at the lookout, silently, silently grouped, catching glimpses as the bride and her mother, not a young mother, carefully wound their way down the stairs toward me and the groom. No grandiose music or the pomp of a bridal party – just the sweetness of John Lennon's "Oh My Love" on a single guitar.

We started by acknowledging the traditional owners – how could you not? This was a borrowed space so completely ours for the time.

Many weddings take place in magnificent settings, which remain a backdrop. But the setting was essence to this wedding, and fittingly articulated in the ceremony.

Other weddings will have music to fill the space when the signing of the documents is taking place – after the vows, after the mar-

riage, in fact. People will chat and celebrate through it. However at this wedding the guitarist sang, before the vows were taken, Leonard Cohen's "Hallelujah", an integral part of the ceremony. More than this – guests were caught up in the event: I recognised the disintegration on the face of a stranger and knew her bereavement; as if the song were not moving enough, someone joined in to the chorus, starting a reaction of spontaneous choral singing I have never before experienced at a wedding.

No church or cathedral could have brought such an atmosphere of awe and connectedness. The hearts of the couple would have been full to bursting. All of this, for them.

When I told my mother about this she said, "And did you sing up too, darling?" "No Mum – I have to stay composed, but inside I was singing. People need you to keep it together as the celebrant; you can't clap your hands with joy or burst into tears, but you can still feel it."

27

In the bush

Tunnelview, Govett's Leap, Gordon Falls,
Narrowneck, King's Tableland, Sublime Point,
Leura Cascades

I've done dozens of weddings at lookouts in the mountains, some more remote than others. I quickly learned that high heels could easily be ruined in such locations! Being married at a lookout usually has a sentimental motive and is a romantic notion in the literal sense – I've seen many weddings become nerve-wracking from a guest's point of view: grandparents negotiating endless rough stairs into the bush, children cavorting on sheer clifftops, high winds, inappropriately clad and shod attendees … Remote wedding locations are beautiful if they are chosen to commemorate a return to a sentimental, personal spot and as such are most moving when the wedding party is intimate – maybe just the couple and their witnesses.

The Victoria and Albert, The Manor House,
Closeburn House, Mt Wilson, Mt Tomah,
Loxley on Bellbird Hill

If you want to take your friends and family to a more accessible world away in the upper mountains, take them up through Bell to Mt Victoria – The Victoria and

Albert is a renowned venue preserved in a charming time-warp, Closeburn House is smaller and more intimate with beautiful gardens and The Manor House is quite majestic: it even snowed here one day while I was conducting a "Jane Austen" themed ceremony.

Mt Wilson also falls into this category. Here the air is crisp and the vegetation ferny and lush, a total contrast to the Aussie bush along the way – in these shadows it can be chilly all year round. Mt Wilson avoids the commercial, popular world and guesthouses with English gardens abound.

And of gardens, almost as far away, is the Mt Tomah Botanic Garden. Of course this is a public space and you have to share it, but there are enough private corners available for weddings here. I've done many weddings at Mt Tomah, from the manicured garden at the top, to the "beach" half-way down, and to the gazebo right at the bottom, to which you are conveyed by groundsmen in a little bus.

Further down the mountain you will find Loxley on Bellbird Hill at Kurrajong, a gorgeous property with views across the plains towards the city. It has accommodation, a superb restaurant with designated wedding terrace and even an in-house violinist: it is the perfect one-stop wedding experience.

28

Mountain icons

Yester Grange, The Mountain Heritage,
The Carrington, The Hydro Majestic, The Fairmont

It was becoming a regular at more of the fine properties in the upper mountains that made me feel I had made it as a celebrant in 2000. One such place is Yester Grange at Wentworth Falls, a unique heritage-listed property with grounds and a view like no other. Couples who marry here are indeed privileged. In that family of properties is the Mountain Heritage, also with lovely views and a cosy, beautifully appointed ambience.

The Carrington Hotel is an icon of Katoomba and has options for indoor and outdoor weddings: on a warm afternoon the front terrace is ideal; on a winter day the lounge with its lead-light windows makes a fine informal chapel.

Another icon with a rich history of luxury and weekend escapades is the faithfully restored Hydro Majestic (I did the first wedding there after the re-opening). I did a lot of weddings there in the early days: in all its forms, the Hydro at Medlow Bath has always had a nostalgic, magnetic charm. Nowadays, it is part of the Escarpment Group of hotels, for whom I am a preferred celebrant.

Less nostalgic but also luxurious is the Fairmont Resort – over the years the options for weddings there have expanded to include garden, gazebo, lakeside and indoor contingencies.

29
Gardens, slopes and plains

Solitary, Jemby Rinjah, The Waldorf Leura,
The Rhododendron Gardens, Buttenshaw Park,
Castlereagh Hall, Hawkesbury Race Club,
Nepean Shores

Three diverse wedding venues up the mountains are Solitary on Cliff Drive, Katoomba, Jemby Rinjah on the way to Evans Lookout at Blackheath and the Waldorf Resort in Leura.

Solitary is a restaurant perched on the bend of Cliff Drive heading up to Katoomba – the legendary Sophie's Fork and View in the '80s. The food is fantastique and weddings are held in the garden overlooking the valley. It always seems quiet and intimate here despite the road winding just beneath.

Then Jemby Rinjah – this is an "eco-resort" right in the bush on Evans Lookout Road. It is very friendly and accommodating, rustic and natural. I've done weddings on the verandahs here, or at the lookout with the reception at the resort afterward.

The Waldorf is a huge motel complex in Leura and has one of the most charming and suitable wedding gardens around – couples can be married "Unter den Linden" – under the stunning lime tree.

Weddings in public parks are a nice option too, although you run the risk of a public spectacle depending on the day and time you choose. The Rhododendron Gardens at Blackheath have been popular for generations and stunning in late spring, while Buttenshaw Park at Springwood is a huge garden with natural, floral terraces making perfect wedding aisles.

If hiring a hall for your wedding (and bringing in your own catering) appeals you couldn't do better than Castlereagh Hall on the road between Penrith and Windsor – there is a lovely wedding area behind the hall and the stretch of pastureland before the foothills is stunning and peaceful. Speaking of stretches of green, a wedding at the Hawkesbury Race Club is a lovely experience in the late afternoon – shadows across the track – and Nepean Shores is a riverside resort and residential complex along the river in Penrith with a wedding garden and facilities for a reception.

Chapter 5
Writing your Ceremony

30

Why "A Ceremony by Design?"

"A Ceremony by Design" is called so for a reason – your wedding ceremony is your design, it's unique. I also added to all my material "… true to your relationship …", because I want you to have your own ceremony, one that will make you think: *Yes! That's us exactly!*

You have to be faithful to what you think makes you tick as a couple. Your ceremony is your opportunity to encapsulate what you honour most in your relationship.

My job as a celebrant is to give you this freedom to be yourselves, while making sure you adhere to the rules which you must obey by law. However, these are separate and you can build your ceremony around them. So whether you want a quiet, touching ceremony that doesn't draw too much attention to the private nature of your relationship, or whether you want to go over the top and scream your commitment from the rooftops – you can have just that. There are just a few simple legalities that absolutely must be included but the rest of the words can be custom-written, bespoke. Even the structure of the ceremony can be played with. So I invite you to alter the sequence a bit to make your ceremony truly unique – it will be my responsibility to make sure the legal part follows a logical sequence.

31

How to begin writing your ceremony

I'll give you lots of ceremonies – of course you can just choose one or mix and match the elements but the whole point of the civil way of being married is that you have the opportunity to make it utterly personal and unique. There is no standard wording you must stick to – so you can look at some models and use your own words.

You start with an introduction. Well, you *can* start with an introduction – but why not just have someone step forward unannounced and deliver a reading or a poem? Something that will arrest the attention of your guests and set the scene for what is to follow, a poem that speaks of love and commitment as you see it, a poem that sums you up, something written so perfectly that you chose it because it struck a chord and said what you were feeling but couldn't put into words?

Then I – or someone else, it doesn't even have to be the celebrant – can come forward and welcome everybody, thank them for coming and more or less state the obvious – why we are here, what has brought you as a couple to this point of marriage. The introduction can tell a little of your story – or a lot, depending on how public you want to be with your relationship. There is no sermon in a civil ceremony, no lesson that someone outside your relationship has a right or obligation to get across – but in the introduction you have the opportunity to talk about what love and commitment mean to you and why you feel it appropriate to express this in a ceremony before your friends and family.

You obviously believe that marriage will make a difference to your relationship – whether it comes after years of waiting, or after the making of a family, or out of a rush of passion and certainty that this is right and irreversible.

Think about what your relationship means to you: your introduction is your chance to reflect on this.

32

After the introduction

You set the scene with your introduction and establish a tone for your ceremony. Usually the introduction is conducted by me as celebrant but do remember anybody can introduce the proceedings and you may prefer to have someone who knows you well – or even do it yourselves. Then you can introduce me later for the official part.

Most couples choose a reading to follow the introduction – I've collated readings and cross-referenced them to parts of the ceremony which they reflect. So this first reading would be about what love, marriage, commitment or your relationship means to you. It can be something you choose that resonates with you and follows on from the sentiments expressed in your introduction.

As with the introduction, readings don't have to be delivered by me. If you want to involve friends and family the readings are an opportunity to honour them as they support you – so ask around: it is a touching mutual gift.

After the introduction comes a crucial part of the ceremony – the recitation from the Marriage Act, stating the contract that you are about to enter into together. This is one of the mandatory parts of the civil marriage ceremony and must be delivered by me. If I haven't been part of the ceremony yet this is where you would introduce me.

These are the words I am obliged to say before we continue. No omissions, no additions – this is what I must say by law:

> "My name is Susan Artup, a Marriage Celebrant duly authorised by law to solemnise marriages according to law. Before you are joined in marriage in my presence and in the presence of these witnesses, I am to remind you of the solemn and binding nature of the relationship into which you are about to enter. Marriage, according to law in Australia, is the union of two people to the exclusion of all others, voluntarily entered into for life."

33

Speak now or forever hold your peace

We don't say that in Australian wedding ceremonies – the statutory declaration that you sign before you can be married takes care of this clause. However, hearing the words from the Marriage Act clears the way for the ceremony to proceed, as does the "Giving Away", which albeit optional and archaic serves as a precursor to the next, more pertinent question, "Do you take …?"

The "Giving Away" is sometimes called the "Presentation" and doesn't have to be conferred by the bride's father – rather it is an opportunity for anybody, friend or family, to speak on behalf of everyone in support of the marriage. It is a kind of blessing then – in fact all the guests can answer "We do!".

A bride can be "given away" by both parents, mother, brother, son, daughter, children … or not "given away" at all. This step is entirely optional. But before discounting it, consider what it adds to the ceremony to include this stage in the sequence leading up to the vows.

The "Giving Away" leads into the next optional question – this one is arresting, spine-tingling, the crux of the matter … in my material there are many variations of the "Asking". It is the "Do you take …?" or the "Will you …?" question – and the answer must be affirmative. You do. You will. That's why you are here.

34

As long as we both shall live

The vows are the essence of the ceremony – they make the marriage complete.

In every civil ceremony I encourage couples to write or choose their own vows.

I have many you can choose from but you are strongly encouraged to put together your own promise of future commitment. The vows may refer to your personal circumstances, allude to secrets between you or shared with your nearest and dearest, or fulfil your role as parents … so give some time to think about what you are actually promising each other. It is the foundation of your life together. This is your commitment.

These personal vows, however, are not enough in themselves to make your marriage legal.

This is what you have to say before me and two witnesses to make a marriage:

> "I (full name) call upon the persons here present to witness that I take you (full name) to be my lawful (wedded) wife (or husband, spouse or partner in marriage), as appropriate."

These are the "legal vows".

As soon as you've said this to each other *you are married*. Even without signing documents, even if your marriage is not registered, you are married – no turning back!

Next you can exchange rings – or one ring – or none: this step is optional but integral to a wedding ceremony. Usually the exchange of rings comes as a discrete step after the vows and can involve a ring-bearer or best man – i.e. it can give someone you love a role to play in the ceremony in stepping forward to present you with the rings. In this, it is an honour – to entrust someone with your wedding bands. Sometimes though the rings are exchanged during the delivery of the personal vows – it just seems to follow nicely. In this case it works if you just produce the ring you have been keeping for each other in a pocket or purse.

It is the exchange of rings that is the culmination of the ceremony: the moment your guests have been waiting for, because straight after follows the public announcement of you as two individuals, united for life in law.

Congratulations!

35
Legally wed!

Although you are married the minute you have exchanged the legal vows (and I love that moment of transition as only we three know it's happened), it is tradition to hold off announcing your marriage until after the rings are exchanged.

Once this has happened I can turn to your guests and pronounce you husband and wife or wife and wife or husband and husband or spouses or married partners. If in fact that is what you want me to announce. I need just say "Congratulations" – but it is nice to enjoy a moment when your change in status is defined. This is the moment when your commitment in marriage is declared and your intent to live together in marriage is cemented – you can play around with the words if you want to get away from tradition.

However, it is after this declaration that I say "You may kiss (the bride)!" – a moment everyone seems to be waiting for. Again this is optional – you can leave it out or say something different.

After the applause dies down you sit quietly to complete the legal formalities – i.e. sign the documents. You and your two witnesses over the age of 18 must sign three documents in my presence: an elegant, commemorative certificate which you keep (proof and souvenir of your marriage), the register (the celebrant's book) and an ordinary-looking form which is your official Certificate of

Marriage that goes to Births Deaths and Marriages. You will sign all three in your existing name. At BDM your official Certificate is processed along with your Notice of Intended Marriage. You can apply for a copy of the Certificate (i.e. purchase it) from BDM. It is essential to get this copy as it is proof not only of your marriage but of your ID. You will need it if you have to prove your identity – e.g. when changing a name on legal documents like licences and passports. It is also worth mentioning that there is no obligation for a woman to change her family name after marriage. Getting a copy of your official Certificate of Marriage keeps your options open. For men as well as women.

After the signing is complete you are introduced to your guests as "Mr and Mrs", "Mr and Mr", "Mrs and Mrs", "a married couple", "married partners" – or however you choose – and usually you will walk back down the aisle or just step forward to meet your guests who will be wanting to congratulate you.

36

Music in your ceremony

There are standard elements to a typical civil wedding ceremony and you can mix and match these to create a unique experience. However, it is what goes in between the scripted lines that really bespeaks your wishes:

> "The inclusion of music in your ceremony can add a dimension of emotion that words alone cannot. Your choice of music will depend on whether you want to give a touch of grandeur to your wedding, or whether you simply wish to reflect the joy of the occasion with music that is special to you."

It is usually you, the couple, who provide the music and ask one of your guests to cue it in. On rare occasions people ask me if I take care of the music at weddings. I don't and this is why: the celebrant is not the stage-manager of the dramatic effects of a wedding, but the facilitator of the legal process of marriage. To that end I take control of the running order of your ceremony, introducing the parts and the readers and so on. It is better if you appoint someone else to take charge of actually turning on the music, fading it out, and stopping it – someone who can work in with me and do this at appropriate times. While in many respects the ceremony is like a piece of theatre, it is not – it is a precise ritual embedded in a serious aspect of law.

While you can use recorded music there are some

moving options if your prefer something live:

> "Some couples choose a string quartet or trio to create a serene atmosphere while guests wait for the ceremony to begin, after which the bride processes to a more ceremonial piece. Sometimes a harpist or vocalist with a guitar can create the required atmosphere. If you have a singer amongst your friends or family it is beautiful to have a song for guests to listen to while you are signing the documents."

Without some music there is nothing to mark the beginning and end of your ceremony – it seems a little strange for wedding parties to emerge out of silence: an audience needs something to mark the moment when they need to stop mingling and pay attention. A specially chosen piece of music or song indicates that something is about to begin, then may be changed to something else for the entrance. Then it is nice to have something to fill the space when the signing of the documents is done. And at the end when it is all over and your marriage is announced it is beautiful to have something triumphant and happy to uplift your guests as they crowd around to congratulate you.

There is an endless and changing number of contemporary songs ideal for weddings, and in my material I list some of the popular classical choices – just to get you started on what you may want.

37

Stage management

Ages ago before I became a marriage celebrant I heard about a couple who had rehearsed their marriage ceremony. Rehearsed? I thought to myself. What? Why? Why would you have to rehearse this special moment? Wouldn't rehearsing fundamentally flaw it? Ruin the very *moment* of it? Surely you make those vows, say those words, stand there trembling with the emotion of it *once* in your life! Isn't that what makes getting married so special? Isn't that why it is *unique*? That you do it once and let the nerves, the emotions, the little slips and glitches flow over and eddy around as part of the essence of your special day?

And when I first became a celebrant no-one ever talked about *the rehearsal*. No-one asked for it, no-one mentioned it. Nowadays, however, bridal magazines and publicity for celebrants put the rehearsal out as de rigueur. Do you conduct a rehearsal? Some couples ask, as advised by whatever source they are quoting. Most couples, in my experience, don't require a rehearsal, and it is quite enough for most to front-up once for this little piece of private theatre that is their wedding ceremony.

I am confident that after we have met and you have the resources I give you at your fingertips, you won't need a rehearsal.

This is my response when people ask me about rehearsals – maybe it is not politically correct but it is the truth:

> "If, after you've met with me and discussed your ceremony, chosen it and feel comfortable with it, you feel you need a rehearsal at the site of your wedding, there is a fee for that, accrued because of extra time and travel. You would also need to give me a month's notice of this.
>
> However, to run through your ceremony wording in my office (and feel free to bring your bridal party) – that is all part of my fee and would take place at the second meeting after your initial booking.
>
> You might still like to go on site some time with your bridal party to practise walking in (in heels) and knowing where to stand and timing your entrance song if you're having one.
>
> All of this can be relayed to me because basically I will do what you tell me."

38
Design template

Here is a design template for your wedding – too easy!

The average civil ceremony will take just under half an hour – including a couple of readings and the signing of documents. It will print out on about two A4 pages.

You will note there are only two sections which by law must be included – verbatim.

The rest is up to you, so enjoy putting together your "ceremony by design".

Introduction
About 200 words containing a welcome and words on marriage

Optional Reading
Something that resonates with you about your relationship

The Marriage Act (obligatory)

Optional Reading
About the meaning of marriage, love or commitment in society

Giving Away (optional)

Asking (optional)

Optional Reading
A personal love poem

Your Own Vows (optional)

The Legal Vows (obligatory)

Exchange of Rings (optional)

Optional Reading
About the symbolism of the rings, the pact that has just been made

Proclamation of Marriage

Signing of the Documents

Optional Reading
A blessing

Presentation
As a married couple

Chapter 6
Special Touches

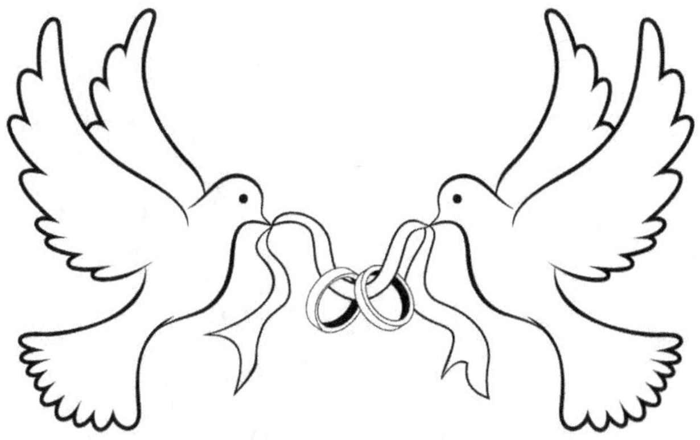

39

Acknowledging Indigenous Custodians

In this chapter I want to tell you about some real variations on conventional design.

To acknowledge traditional owners should not be a variation, in fact it is surprising that so few people elect to start their ceremony with an Acknowledgement of Country. Often wedding ceremonies are held in stunning outdoor natural surroundings which beg acknowledgement of the earth beneath our feet, and its history.

So if you want to do this, you will research who the traditional owners of your wedding location are and begin your ceremony by stating that you acknowledge them, their land and traditions.

You can leave it at that or go on to state your respect of Aboriginal Elders past and present who are custodians of culture, hopes and memories for future generations.

In my material I give you examples of words which may be said.

40

Acknowledging Children

These days a marriage ceremony is not always solely the legalisation of the union between two people but the formal consolidation of a family: whether it is of children shared by the couple or of a merging of two former, independent families.

While the primary relationship to be celebrated at a wedding is that between the spouses, the importance of children can be acknowledged as a natural step in the ceremony.

So if the couple has been living as parents with their own kids the "marriage" is one for the whole family; if they have been living in a blended family, the ceremony is an opportunity to welcome the other's children and acknowledge them, even thank them for accepting a new parent.

There are lots of ways to ritualise different family circumstances to involve offspring no matter what age — older kids can witness, "give away" or do readings, young children can be spoken about in the ceremony (even in the vows a commitment to them can be made), light candles, accept symbolic gifts … as with the rest of the ceremony, you are only limited by your imagination.

Here is one example which acknowledges step-children:

> "________ and ________ would also like to acknowledge the support and role of their

children. When two people come together and bring with them children of their own, there are concerns and challenges of each. Sharing a parent with another child, learning to live with a new person, learning the differences in attitudes and ways of life. It has been a growing time for each of the children and ________ and ________ would like to say thank you to ________ and ________ for the way they have accepted ________ and ________ as part of their lives."

41

The Unity Candle

The lighting of candles is a powerful symbol in all kinds of rituals. If you don't want to be too elaborate with your words, the quiet lighting of a candle speaks volumes and sets a tone of reverence, respect, thankfulness – it has the dramatic effect of setting the scene. It also means you can acknowledge people by giving them a part to play in your ceremony.

The idea of a Unity Candle is to symbolise a new beginning. Sometimes two smaller candles can be lit first to symbolise the two separate lives coming together in commitment to each other. Then from these two candles the Unity Candle is lit.

The two candles can be lit by the mothers as a symbol of the families from which the couples come, or by the parties to marriage, or by the best man and matron of honour. Of course, anyone can light the candles. Or one candle – a grandmother/father, family friend, child, celebrant can come forward and light the candle – like in a church service, at the beginning, to create the atmosphere and invoke a certain spirit.

And then the text can talk about what the flame represents – a flame now burning undivided from two, or the single light of love and hope … you can say all this, or nothing at all.

The drawback is that candles don't stay lit outdoors, so try candles with glass domes around them.

42

The Ceremony of the Roses

In the Ceremony of the Roses a couple exchanges roses as a symbol of love. All flowers have symbolic significance but the rose is the symbol of love and was included in ceremonies of a bygone age.

There are several variations of this ceremony in which roses are exchanged by the bride and groom. In one ceremony, the couple exchanged a white and a red rose each.

The white rose, I said to them, was a "symbol of your larger understandings, of your spiritual nature and your spiritual truth ... standing for the purity of your real and highest self and the purity of God's love."

The red rose, I continued, was a "symbol of your individual understandings of earthly things, that you both know and agree how life will be with you in bodily form and within the physical structure called marriage. Give these roses now to each other as a symbol of your sharing of these agreements and understandings with love."

Of course you don't have to say *these* words, or any words at all.

The roses can be exchanged before or after the rings are exchanged – or at any time where this would be smoothest and most meaningful.

A vase of water, symbol of life, can be provided for the roses after they are exchanged; the rings can be tied to the stems of the roses.

As part of the ceremony you could suggest that roses be a symbol of love, conciliation or apology at times when words fail to heal in difficult or challenging times ahead.

43

Sharing the Chalice

I used this ceremony in one of my first weddings over 20 years ago.

The chalice of wine holds very strong symbolism – Holy Communion, the Last Supper, promises exchanged, commitment sealed, good will and trust. In ancient rites it is the representative of the Divine Female, the Cup of Life.

In this ceremony the couple was invited to share from the cup in their first sip as husband and wife after the rings were exchanged.

Words to the effect of this symbolism can be chosen and recited for the occasion.

The mothers of the parties to marriage can come forward to fill the chalice while the ritual is explained.

Then one partner can offer it to the other and vice-versa.

A ritual like this can be included in a ceremony if you prefer it to readings of poetry.

44

The Silken Ribbon

This ritual is German in origin and could be included as a blessing toward the end or as a precursor to the commitment in the exchange of vows. So after the Asking and before the Vows. It is beautifully symbolic and adds a unique touch.

In this ritual the celebrant takes a blue silken ribbon and places it over the shoulders of the couple, and recites a poem which describes the ribbon as a symbol of unity which entwines two lives as they join in facing the joys and challenges of life.

Then the ribbon can remain over their shoulders while the vows are exchanged and ceremoniously removed and handed to someone in the party for safekeeping.

45

The Sand Ceremony

This is a symbolic, interactive element of a wedding ceremony. There are many variations but basically the bride and groom each takes a small container of coloured sand and taking turns tips it into one larger container. The idea is that the two separate jars represent two separate lives which are now joined into one in the larger jar. The sands are of contrasting colours, which poured together have an interesting, decorative effect which alters over time as the sands settle. To this end, a specially chosen container should be sourced as the result is an ornament and a keepsake.

Sand has many representations: the foundation of the lives the couple comes from, a means of measuring time "like sand through an hourglass", the grains which accumulate to create experience, a souvenir of a favourite beach …

In a ceremony I did recently the couple used three layers of sand. At first we had three separate containers: as the celebrant I was to pour the first layer of sand (white in this case) to symbolise the foundation of the marriage. Then the couple poured their sand (chocolate brown and russet) in turn, a little at a time, and a pattern emerged. The two colours now blending as a symbol of two people joining forever in love.

Then I poured a last layer of sand to represent the community of family and friends supporting the marriage and holding the couple together. Although the sand may move around in the vase and the colours may shift and blend in new ways, the grains of sand can never again be separated. The wish is that the couple's union will be as eternal and inseparable as the grains of sand in their vase.

Sand can be used effectively too when children are involved to symbolise the joining and creation of families – then many colours can be used and the children can play a part in the ceremony.

46

The Ring Warming

Warming the rings is a lovely ritual best suited to smaller weddings, as timing is of the essence. The idea is that you pass your wedding rings around your wedding guests so that everyone can hold them in the palm of their hands and imbue them with good wishes, love and energy. With all these positives from the hearts of your nearest and dearest, how could your marriage not be off to a good start? This is a really unobtrusive ritual. If you don't want to make a fuss but you do want something inclusive and interactive, a Ring Warming is a subtle and memorable addition. You should decide who should begin the process though and where the rings should end up – just before you exchange vows. So you should put someone in charge of keeping an eye on the rings' journey and be ready to catch them at the end and bring them forward. For example an attendant of the bride or matron of honour could start it off and an attendant of the groom or best man could end up with the rings and as tradition would have it hold them for the presentation of rings step.

There's also an anonymous reading that goes well with this ritual – it's called "Endlessness" and talks of wedding bands as symbols of continuity and value, reflecting love with no end. I can give it to you.

If you don't want an elaborate ceremony maybe just this touch would be enough.

47

The Irish Wedding Cup

This is a variation on Sharing the Chalice – but you could have this after the signing is done to close the ceremony as it involves all the guests in celebration. In this way you are not only re-booting the ceremony after the documents but also spontaneously starting the party, which is often a bit awkward because people don't know when to move along after the formal part is done.

This ritual involves the couple sharing wine and drinking to their relationship.

It can go like this:

> "This wine-filled chalice symbolises the cup of life with all its sweetness, made sweeter because now you will drink from it together. Bitterness, disappointment, obstacles and sorrows will be fewer because you share them. Drinking from this same cup symbolises the pledges you have made to one another to share life without knowing what may come your way, only that you will lend your strength and support to one another. As you drink from this one cup, so have you become united.
> Now drink to the love you've shared in the past."

Couple sips from the cup.

> "Drink to your love in the present, on this your wedding day."

Couple sips from the cup.

Celebrant invites all to join in drinking to the bride and groom:

> "Let us drink to your love in the future and forever!"

Couple sips from the cup and hands it back.

> "As you have shared the wine, so may you share your lives. May you go forward in life to face its joys and challenges together. May you see opportunities and seize them. May you maintain the understanding to yield when needed, while keeping the constancy of your devotion."

48

The Wine and the Wooden Box

This is thought to be a Dutch tradition. The couple should find a wooden box that will hold a bottle of wine and two wine glasses. They should then write one another a letter with the reasons they fell in love, describing the qualities they find most endearing in the other. In fact, a love letter. The letters should not be read but sealed and placed in the box with the wine. As part of the ceremony the box should be nailed shut. The idea is that should the couple find their marriage in trouble down the track, they should open the wine, drink it together and read their letters. Together or apart. Keepsakes from the wedding day could be included too – photos, pressed flowers – the ceremony even. The vows.

My aim is to set all my couples off on a path of bliss so if the marriage sails clearly, they have permission to open the box on their twenty-fifth anniversary and save the wine!

This ritual can come right at the end of the ceremony – after the signing – the last step of the ceremony then would be the hammering in of the last nail.

I would explain the ritual to the guests before the signing, then after invite the couple to place the letters in the box and take it in turns to hammer in the nails.

It's a dramatic end to a wedding ceremony!

49
The Seven Steps

Civil marriage ceremonies are underpinned by freedom – the opportunity to compose your ceremony with a minimum of rules. I can give you guidelines but if you want a unique ceremony it is up to you to create it from ideas you have come across and convictions you have held … so your ceremony can be an eclectic mix of cultural elements, religious aspects, personal references … and they don't need to be exact or consistent: a little of this, a little of that will be OK. Civil ceremonies do not purport to represent any particular culture or religion so you can mix it up to include your favourite touches.

The Seven Steps was adapted by a couple I married years ago – their ceremony was "An Indian Vedic Ceremony in the Tradition of Sapthapadi". The Seven Steps were incorporated within their vows and involved the couple circling a Unity Candle.

Traditionally this ritual is more prescribed, but for my couple it unfolded thus, as the couple repeated with each step around the candle:

> "We take this first step to live together with cooperation and understanding.
> We take this second step to grow together in physical, emotional and spiritual strength.
> We take this third step to communicate truthfully and openly with one another.
> We take this fourth step to be generous with

our material wealth.
We take this fifth step to welcome children
into our lives.
We take this sixth step to work for harmony in
our relationship and in our community.
We take this seventh step to walk together as
lifelong friends."

I liked this ritual – thoughtful and a little different for western weddings.

50

The Hand Blessing Ceremony

This one gets to me every time. It can be incorporated into the ceremony any time from just before the vows are taken to the final words.

In it you should take it in turns to hold each other's hands, palms up, and look into them, the hands of your soul mate. The hands are the symbol of protection, shelter and guidance for whatever you may face in years ahead. In this, you bless each other's hands so that they may have the strength and tenderness to fulfil your vows of marriage.

The Hand Blessing can take the place of a reading. I ask you to acknowledge the gift that taking your partner's hands symbolises – on your wedding day they are young and strong with the promise of your future together. Your partner's hands will work with you, cherish and support you. They will grow old with your hands and their touch will comfort you even when you are old and grey.

The exact words are in the books I will give you when we are working on your ceremony.

51
The Handfasting Ceremony

The Handfasting Ceremony can be included in a ceremony with the Hand Blessing words – if one does not detract from the other.

There are variations of handfasting. In two of these, you need either six ribbons or one wider one and a special pouch or box to keep the "fast", or tied, ribbons in for eternity.

This ritual can be incorporated either before or after the exchange of rings and can include some interactive questions, although if that is not your style it doesn't have to.

Here is an example:

Celebrant:

> "Now you have exchanged rings as a symbol of the union you have made. As a further symbol of this bond, you are crossing your hands right hand to right hand and left hand to left hand, and declaring before your family and friends your intention to be joined forever in marriage. Today's promises will be held in these ribbons, tied together as you grow together.
>
> Do you both agree to the Handfasting Ceremony?"

Couple:

> "We do"

The celebrant ties the light blue ribbon, symbol of the sharing of burdens. The couple is asked to accept this, and the binding is made. The process continues through the binding of five more ribbons: the silver ribbon, symbol of hopes and dreams, the red ribbon, symbol of enduring passion, the green ribbon, symbol of joy and laughter, the white ribbon, symbol of peace, and the dark blue ribbon, symbol of strength against adversity. There are six bindings, six questions.

The six ribbons are tied then together in a single knot on top of the hands. The knot is twice tied so that it remains so when the hands are taken away.

The binding of hands symbolises the union of love and trust.

When the hands are removed from the ribbons the knot that remains is placed in a pouch to stay forever tied as a reminder of these promises.

This is quite a dramatic ceremony in itself and can be simplified into the version where one wide, luxurious ribbon is used and the questions and answers are just replaced by a commentary from the celebrant.

It works really well either way.

52

Blessing Stones or Shells

Almost any item can be given symbolic significance. This ritual is perfect for a natural setting: the exchanging of stones or shells by the couple, coloured or inscribed, instead of, or as well as, rings. The stones are cast by the newly-weds into the sea or a river to symbolise their unity during the ebb and flow of their lives together.

Something like this can be said:

> "These stones and your love are as enduring as the earth itself; they will withstand the tides of the sea and of life. The dreams and secrets of your love are as deep as the ocean. Please cast your stones into the water."

A variation on this is to provide a bowl of coloured stones for guests to take. The guests are invited to write a wish on a card, read it out and cast their stones into the water.

The same can be done with shells at a beach wedding.

This ceremony can be accompanied by an appropriate reading.

53
Releasing Butterflies

This is a stunning symbol as the finale to a ceremony – after everything, including the signing of the documents, is over – the instant after you are introduced as Mr and Mrs or married partners or a married couple.

Obviously butterflies must be released outside so if your ceremony is outdoors it is ideal. If not there has to be some choreography to get you to the exit, followed by guests. At some stage everyone is handed a little packet of comatose butterflies which is not to be opened until the given moment. Then the butterflies come to life and soar off in all directions. After the celebrant explains the symbolism of the butterflies the couple makes the first wish and release and the guests are then invited to make a wish and release theirs. According to native American legend, a randomly captured butterfly can make a wish come true. By releasing the butterfly you are ensuring that your wish is taken to the heavens and granted.

The release of the butterflies can be accompanied by something like:

> "... as the butterflies fly to the light may your love soar on their wings to a bright future of hope and promise ... may we remember this moment of freedom and possibilities even as these creatures are carried on the air to unknown adventures!"

It's a lovely way to involve your guests. Just be gentle with the little creatures!

54

Releasing Doves

Another symbolic finale to a ceremony is the release of doves. I have seen this one work beautifully at commitments, namings and funerals as well.

There are a couple of businesses in Sydney who keep and train doves just for this — to fly off from a wedding venue and return home to their owners.

Doves are a symbol of peace, love and new beginnings — and they fly in pairs.

They may fly in separate directions but at night they return home to their partner.

These are words that can be said by the celebrant:

> "You begin your life as a devoted and loving married couple. May the releasing of this pair of doves symbolise the beginning of your new life journey, taken together.
> May the inspiration of the doves, which bond together for life, be with you as you combine your lives in never-ending love.
> We wish for you that your life together will be long, rich and rewarding and that your marriage will carry everything that we see represented in the doves."

Chapter 7
"Theme" Weddings

55
"Pagan" ceremony

Many couples take advantage of the opportunity to author a unique ceremony by adopting a theme which better suits their style and beliefs than a conventional ceremony. Almost anything goes as long as the sections of the Marriage Act are adhered to.

When a theme is adopted it too can be changed and moulded to create a unique ritual. Themes can be adapted, borrowed, re-constituted: nothing is strict.

I have conducted some "pagan" ceremonies. In one, elements of nature were invoked and friends played a part in addressing the couple, asking questions and eliciting answers as to their intent to commit. The ceremony was conducted at dawn at Evans Lookout at Blackheath and was really lovely: the first rays of the sun fell across the bride's face as the vows were exchanged.

This ceremony is scripted in my wedding material and begins by calling upon the energies of the Feminine and Masculine, acknowledging that these energies are fluid and interplay to create a union and a future.

The language is full of metaphor and is dense and formal. The simple "Do you take?" question is replaced by five longer questions from friends. After every answer, a blessing is given, in which the Sun, Moon, Air, Water, Fire, Time and the Seasons are called upon to safeguard the marriage as it is absorbed into the Mystery of Life.

When the rings are exchanged reference is made to the symbolism of continuing changing seasons within this mystery. The bride and groom bring the symbols of their love-light by lighting a single candle from their two separate candles.

A similar tone is taken in the proclamation of the couple as husband and wife and the ceremony is concluded fittingly.

It is possible to weave the modern requirements of the Marriage Act through this "pagan" theme to create a unique, legal ceremony of marriage.

56
Polytheistic ceremony

This ceremony was also presented as a "pagan" ceremony. It focuses on the power and awe of creation, the place of humankind, and the connection of two souls within the universe. In place of religion it contemplates universal laws. So if you want to make a more serious statement in your ceremony, this might be for you. It relies on ideas and words which can be integrated with the legal wording of marriage. So add to this the sections required of the Marriage Act and your introduction could talk about marriage being the union of two souls according to any beliefs and cultures.

Marriage, you can say, brings with it strength and wisdom and is declared under the universal law of life. This law is founded on love, which guides life and transcends death. Love is the foundation of creation.

Instead of the traditional "giving away", I would directly ask the bride for her consent to the marriage – and her family would be asked for their blessings.

Then when the wedding takes place, you would join hands and I would remind you that your marriage should be as firm as the earth beneath you and as constant as the stars above.

I would tell you to be guided in knowledge by the strength of your mind and will; to be guided in happiness by your desire and devotion. I would tell you to be patient and understanding and to give each other time and space to grow. Above all I would tell you to be generous and affectionate and confident in your partnership to bring you comfort and ease.

Instead of the traditional "I do" answer, I would ask each of you a question, to which you would reply: "It is my wish".

Your personal vows would use the words "thee", "thy" and "thou" and make spiritual references seamlessly followed by the legal commitment.

There is a full version of this ceremony in my material.

57

Jane Austen ceremony

Although stage management is very important, a wedding ceremony isn't supposed to be a piece of theatre. Using a theme for your wedding ceremony just gives it an alternative slant. The crux of the wedding is the commitment, not the theme.

Usually the theme is expressed through dress (you might want your friends to dress a certain way) and the type of language you choose. In this "Jane Austen" wedding, dress, language and symbols were used to create a theme. Not to mention the location and venue! The ceremony took place at the Victoria and Albert Guesthouse – circa 1914 – perfect! This wonderful property is in Mt Victoria in the upper mountains and the season was winter … so cold, and yes, the ceremony was outside and finished just before it started to snow lightly. You couldn't really imagine a ceremony like this anywhere but in the mountains.

Here are some excerpts from this unique ceremony, beginning with a blessing:

> "Today you begin your journey of life shared, bound together by the vows of this ceremony. Your marriage is a partnership founded on the strong bonds of friendship and love. Many are the years you will share and countless the moons you will watch together. This wedding is a symbol, a celebration, a public recognition of what already exists in the silent places of

your hearts. If you keep your vows, your sacred trust, happy will be many of your days."

Both mothers then walked forward as representatives of each family, and lit a single candle each, then returned to their places:

"In this ceremony today we celebrate love, and I begin by offering homage to the eternal flame of sacred love that burns within every loving heart. May the love you have received from your families guide you as you make this commitment to bind your hearts together as one forever."

The celebrant lit some incense:

"Let your love be as incense to the breeze, let it create an ever-growing circle that spreads love and may your union be a thing of beauty to all who behold it. May the fires of love kindle in your passion for each other throughout the years."

The celebrant rang a bell three times:

"Above are the stars, below are the stones. Remember, like a star should your love be constant, like the earth should your love be firm. Possess one another, yet be understanding. Have patience, for storms may come and go. Be free always in giving of affection and warmth."

This style was continued in the Asking, Vows and Rings, with the insertion of the legal commitment.

58

"Buddhist" ceremony

Some time ago I was asked by a couple to conduct a "Buddhist" ceremony. Inverted commas because I am not a monk. So this is less a theme wedding than an alternative approach – which is the hallmark of civil celebrancy. It also demonstrates again the eclectic nature of civil ceremonies.

This is the Buddhist Wedding Address:

"Marriage is perhaps the most important ceremony of life, because ... upon the success of this partnership depends the ability of both husband and wife to give to this world their full creative value as human beings. Through their united resolve before the Gohonzon to create a wonderfully harmonious, yet essentially progressive unit of society ... they draw out from each other the Three Poisons of Anger, Greed, and Stupidity, which might otherwise afflict their family life with misery ... they are able to send out waves of peace and friendship, not only to the community which immediately surrounds them, but the whole country and the whole world.

In the Gosho 'Letter to the Brothers', Nichiren Daishonin wrote: 'When a husband is happy, his wife will be fulfilled. If a husband is a thief, his wife will become one too ... if grass withers; orchids grieve, if pine trees flourish, oaks rejoice.'

The relationship between husband and wife is the foundation of society because not only do they have it in their power to bring fresh new lives into this world, but also their home and family should be, in the words of our Buddhist teacher, 'an open fortress of faith', which is invincible to attack from the outside, yet is open to all who approach in friendship or with seeking minds, a firm base of faith anchored in the great Middle Way of the Gohonzon founded upon trust, from which the family can go forth daily into society, shining with the vital energy, wisdom and compassion which arises from the universal life-force flowing through their lives.

I wish you happiness and fulfilment throughout your lives together and ask you both, before the Gohonzon, never to neglect your daily practice and joyful activities for the future peace and happiness of your family, your friends, and the whole world, basing your lives always on the teachings of Nichiren Daishonin, the Buddha of the true cause.

In the words of the Gosho you should work together like the sun and the moon, a pair of eyes, or the two wings of a bird. With the sun and the moon, how can you fall into the paths of darkness? With a pair of eyes, how can you fail to behold the faces of Shakyamuni, Taho and all the other Buddhas of the universe? With a pair of wings, you will surely be able to fly in an instant to the Buddha's land of eternal happiness."

Chapter 8
Poetry about Marriage

59

Why poetry?

The choice of a couple of poems – or readings – is essential to a wedding ceremony's meaning. A poem can encapsulate feelings with a poignancy and elegance in a way that ordinary conversation cannot. Clumsy, wordy phrases are replaced by eloquence in a few lines with a poem. The allure of poetry is that the words of a stranger, the poet, can so perfectly sum up our personal feelings. That's why some poems become famous and endure through centuries: they are as relevant today as when they were written. Contemporary song lyrics, too, are just as much poetry as are classic sonnets and ballads – they allow the soul its self-expression. Words correctly chosen and used enable us to be "masters of our own mouths" – a description I read recently and share because of its aptness.

Part of the function and process of a traditional wedding ceremony is to call upon blessings from above, from outside this space and time. The vows may be made, but they need to be blessed – hence the epithalamia of ancient times.

What happens in the expression of wedding vows is an earthly binding – but the poetry is something sublime – its role is to invoke a divine blessing, to appeal to eternity to sustain the joy and provide strength through difficult times. It is a blessing which beseeches an unwavering comfort.

You must take responsibility in the ritual promises of marriage, because in them you are creating a union. The poetry you choose calls on external powers to safeguard your union. The poetry sets the seal. Poetry reinforces and blesses the promise, and as a couple this blessing will be fundamental to your very being as you go through life together.

There are limitless versions of modern, personal wedding blessings which resonate with tradition. Tradition is a steadying influence in a relationship – it's up to you to decide what, if anything, you want to take from it.

The poems that you choose should say what you feel about love and the vows you are making. Choosing them makes you think about your ceremony and therefore your marriage. It is an opportunity to think about what marriage means to you.

60
Romantic poetry

People talk about a love affair as a romance, and think of a romantic gesture as an expression of modern love. Romantic poetry is pretty much equated with love poetry and for the purpose of Valentine's Day and sentimental occasions this is probably true and adequate – yet "romantic" has a much looser meaning. "Romantic" really just means something related to fiction, an ideal, story-like situation – both the French and German word for novel is "Roman". Hence the expression "romantic notion" doesn't actually refer to an idea based on love – it is used in the original sense.

However, it is easy to see how the period of Romantic poetry, which began in the eleventh century and wasn't necessarily about sexual love, gave rise to the modern notion of romantic poetry = love poetry that we use in wedding ceremonies today. Romantic poetry was performed by the troubadours as they travelled from court to court in southern France, celebrating courtly love and adventure. "Romance" was the name given to a story in one of the romance languages, notably French. Romances told fictitious tales of chivalry based on limitless imagination and heroic ideals. This was far from the realism of preceding literature. "Romance" came to mean any unreal, improbable or impossible story.

For centuries then "romantic" meant "like the old

romances": fantastic stories of knights, magicians and dragons in an incredible, fanciful, even absurd world. Then the word evolved to mean attractive, alluring and captivating; it began to describe anything which aroused feelings of awe or wonder. Later it came to take on the meanings "magic", "suggestive" or "nostalgic". Finally it came to mean something inexplicable, desirable and irresistible. This "romantic" attraction is what draws you to the one you love.

61

Setting the scene with a poem

Poems for weddings – there is such a range of them. From the classics in language barely recognisable, to the lyrics in the vernacular of 21st century tunes – there is a place for every kind and combination of words. The point of poetry is that it uses a different way, a simpler way, a more elegant way to express the obvious and ordinary.

The poems you choose will have the best impact if you integrate them appropriately – for example at the beginning of the ceremony you are indicating what this commitment means to you. Many, many attempts have been made to define love but words so often fail – you will choose what resonates with you and what clicks. These poems are about the general nature of relationships.

Later, when it comes to making your vows, you could choose a much more personal reading. There are no rules defining love but it is generally accepted that the love which compels you to consolidate your life with your partner's is based on the realisation that being apart is intolerable. And that you want to be together forever.

Love is true. It doesn't change. It adapts. It has no conditions or measures. You can count on it.

This sonnet by William Shakespeare says all this. It is indeed a little overused, but read well, it is a beautiful introduction to commitment:

Sonnet 116

Let me not to the marriage of true minds
Admit impediments. Love is not love
Which alters when it alteration finds,
Or bends with the remover to remove:

O no! It is an ever-fixed mark
That looks on tempests and is never shaken;
It is the star to every wandering bark,
Whose worth's unknown, though his height be taken.

Love's not Time's fool, though rosy lips and cheeks
Within his bending sickle's compass come;
Love alters not with his brief hours and weeks
But bears it out even to the edge of doom.

If this be error and upon me proved.
I never writ nor no man ever loved.

62

When you are meant to be together

The amazing thing about poems written in centuries past, from times whose mores we perceive to be different, is that the words express sentiments *exactly* as we feel them today. In other words, we did not invent passion in our modest lifetimes!

I've referred to poems which attempt to define love and to tell us what to expect and offer in a relationship. They express the general rules of engagement with another person, with a partner. Someone once said to me "you don't marry the person you can live with, but the person you can't live without." Absolutely! You merge your life with the one who complements you in all the things you observe, feel and do.

This poem by Percy Bysshe Shelley was written in 1819. It talks of natural attraction: an irresistible law over which we have no control, which, unfulfilled, lays us to waste. It brims with glorious images, and in the right ceremony, read by the right person, works beautifully as a more personal poem you could include before the vows of marriage are exchanged.

Love's Philosophy

The fountains mingle with the river,
And the rivers mix with the ocean,
The winds of heaven mix forever
With a sweet emotion;

Nothing in the world is single;
All things by law divine
In one another's beings mingle
Why not I with thine?

See the mountains kiss high heaven,
And the waves clasp one another;
No sister flower would be forgiven
If it disdained its brother;

And the sunlight clasps the earth,
And the moonbeams kiss the sea,
What are all these kissings worth
If thou kissed not me?

Shelley was no role-model for marital fidelity. At age nineteen, he eloped with sixteen-year-old Harriet Westbrook. Shelley also became enamored of the philospopher Godwin Wollstonecraft's daughter, Mary, and he left Harriet for her. During a seance it was proposed that each person present should write a ghost story. Mary's contribution to the contest became the novel *Frankenstein*. When Harriet Shelley committed suicide, Shelley and Mary Godwin were married. Shelley lost custody of his two children by Harriet because of his adherence to the notion of free love!

Shortly before his thirtieth birthday, Shelley was drowned in a storm while sailing to Italy in his schooner, the *Don Juan*. Aptly named.

63
Individuality and intimacy

In many of the words written on the definition of loving relationships, "respect for each other's individuality" is a stand-out element. This leads to the question of balance in a relationship: what is more important? To adhere to the self or to blend into the union? Ideal love allows this question and finds the compromise, the complement, the flexibility, the understanding …

Anyway, enough about what love should be.

The love that demands that being apart is intolerable comes from intimacy, not to clinging to an ideal of individuality. This intimacy gives rise to idioms like "you complete me", "you are my other half", "I am only half-living without you".

This is a very dangerous intimacy which makes us vulnerable. To lose that intimacy is the devastation that break-ups deal with. However, it is the element of love that you would die for, to feel as one with your partner in a unique and totally exclusive way.

Sometimes this is an intimacy which you best realise years after being together.

Poems about this feeling can be included in your ceremony, even read by you to each other.

Sonnet 113 by the famous Spanish poet, Pablo Neruda, is one such poem. Another is by the Chinese poet, Kuan Tao Sheng:

Married Love

You and I
Have so much love
That it burns like a fire
In which we bake a lump of clay
Moulded into a figure of you
And a figure of me.
Then we take both of them
And break them into pieces
And mix the pieces with water
And mould again a figure of you
And a figure of me.
I am in your clay.
You are in my clay.

64
Seek and ye shall find

A marriage ceremony is far more than the legalisation of a relationship. This is the public recognition that one's status has changed and is useful if not essential for the practical purposes of life in society.

But one of the things that is fundamental to a wedding ceremony is that it gives individuals the opportunity to celebrate the culmination of their search, to express their sense of personal fulfilment and jubilation in "finding" a compatible other – more than that, a vital other.

A wedding speaks of seeking and finding, yearning and peace. In this, it celebrates the moment. The most beautiful personal love poems are about this and their place in the ceremony is around the time the vows are exchanged.

So the poems defining love and commitment would come first (introducing the ceremony), then the personal pledges (before or after the vows) then the blessings to express hope and well-wishes (right at the end after the rings and signing).

Here are two poems about the search for love and the place of rest real love can bring to individuals. One is an anonymous Hawaiian wedding song:

> *Here all seeking is over,*
> *the lost has been found,*
> *a mate has been found*

> *to share the chills of winter —*
> *now Love asks that you be united.*
> *Here is a place to rest,*
> *a place to sleep,*
> *a place in heaven.*
> *Now two are becoming one,*
> *the black night is shattered,*
> *the eastern sky grows bright.*
> *At last the great day has come!*

The second is by the Persian poet Rumi, who was born in 1207 and is one of the most widely read poets in modern times:

Lovers

> *The minute I heard my first love story*
> *I started looking for you, not knowing*
> *how blind that was.*
>
> *Lovers don't finally meet somewhere.*
> *They're in each other all along.*

65
Commitment

Marriage Joins Two People in the Circle of its Love by Edmund O'Neill is a reading which describes an ideal of marriage. While not exclusive to marriage, it describes integrity brought about by commitment.

In it the poet comments that commitment in marriage is a commitment to life and to being the best we can be. A marital partner will take on a number of roles and relationships.

This union will intensify experiences and understanding and will be renewed and refreshed because of this. Every couple's union is unique; the promises are private and personal and will take a life together to fulfil.

This reading would be effective at the beginning of the ceremony – after or even before the introduction, or at the very end after the commitment – the vows – are complete.

66

Union

Robert Fulghum is an American author the title of whose well-known book is *All I really need to know I learned in Kindergarten*. He was born in 1937.

In 1996, he wrote "Union", an often quoted excerpt which embodies truth, not premise, about being drawn together in marriage.

This truth is that commitment doesn't just happen on the day of your wedding. It is something that builds and is demonstrated in your everyday interactions from the moment you accept to be together, exclusively, forever. This commitment is cemented in all your conversations and plans for the future; you are wedding yourselves together as you travel the path to the public announcement. On the day of your ceremony you are vouching for everything you have said, summing it all up, and even though you will remain the same person to each other things will be different. In your ceremony you will entrust your family and friends – and your celebrant – with the truth that you have been holding in your hearts. And your union will be public, formal and legal.

This reading is really effective right at the beginning of the ceremony – it can be read by a parent or friend, someone who has known the couple for a long time.

67

The truth about love

Bertrand Russell was a British philosopher who wrote about many themes on the human condition in books such as *The Problems of Philosophy* (1912) and *The Conquest of Happiness* (1930). He died in 1970.

Rainer Maria Rilke was an Austrian poet responsible for sublime German lyrical poetry and novels. He died in 1927.

The words of these thinkers are relevant and much quoted still: love, commitment, devotion – truths, defined absolutely.

Pink was not the first to attempt to nail "The Truth about Love" (2014).

Best and most important – Bertrand Russell

It is therefore possible for a civilised man and woman to be happy in marriage, although if this is to be the case a number of conditions must be fulfilled. There must be a feeling of complete equality on both sides; there must be no interference with mutual freedom; there must be the most complete physical and mental intimacy and there must be a certain similarity in regard to standards of values ...

Given all these conditions, I believe marriage to be the best and most important relation that can exist between two human beings.

Letters to a young poet – Rainer Maria Rilke

For one human being to love another human being – that is perhaps the most difficult task entrusted to us, the ultimate task, the final test and proof, the work for which all other work is merely preparation. Loving does not at first mean merging, surrendering and uniting with another person – it is a high inducement for the individual to ripen, to become something in himself, to become world, to become world in himself for the sake of another person; it is a great, demanding claim on him, something that chooses him and calls him to great distances.

68
Permanently settled

I described a ritual called the Seven Steps earlier. This was an adaptation of one of the many Hindu wedding rituals, which invoke blessings of happiness, harmony and growth.

As in western culture, a marriage ceremony in Hindu tradition is a rite which enables two individuals to begin their journey through life together. The ceremony blesses this journey and establishes the union of spirit and matter so that a future of serenity and stability is possible. The Seven Steps symbolises the beginning of the journey, each step representing a vow of marriage.

This anonymous reading has sublimity and earthliness:

> *We have taken the Seven Steps. You have become mine forever.*
> *Yes, we have become partners. I have become yours. Hereafter, I cannot live without you. Do not live without me. Let us share the joys. We are word and meaning, united.*
> *You are thought and I am sound.*
> *May the nights be honey sweet for us; may the mornings be honey-sweet for us; may the earth be honey-sweet for us; may the heavens be honey-sweet for us. May the plants be honey-sweet for us; may the cows yield us honey-sweet milk!*
> *As the heavens are stable, as the earth is stable, as the mountains are stable, as the*

> *whole universe is stable, so may our union be permanently settled.*

Of course you don't have to have an Indian ceremony to include this and you don't have to perform the Seven Steps … just omit the first sentence!

69
Honey-sweet love

"Honey-sweet": words redolent of gentle fulfilment and serenity. The last reading I shared from an Indian Vedic ceremony described the new marital state with these words.

Milk, honey, wine, dates are all symbols of plenty, celebration, wholeness and gratitude. These two poems, one from Rumi, and one, anonymous, from Ancient Egypt, are stunning in their simplicity:

This Love

This love is as good
as oil and honey to the throat
as linen to the body,
as fine garments to the gods,
as incense to worshippers
when they enter in,
as the little seal-ring
to my finger.
It is like a ripe pear
in a man's hand,
it is like dates
we mix with wine,
it is like seeds
the baker adds to bread.
We will be together
even when old age comes.

And the days in between
will be food set before us,
dates and honey, bread and wine.

This Marriage – Rumi

This marriage be wine with halvah, honey dissolving in milk.
This marriage be the leaves and fruit of a date tree.
This marriage be women laughing together for days on end.
This marriage, a sign for us to study.
This marriage, beauty.
This marriage, a moon in a light blue sky.
This marriage, this silence fully mixed with spirit.

Chapter 9
What is Love anyway?

70

Sweet mystery of life

"Ah, sweet mystery of life ... at last I've found you!" – in the '70s my *camp* friends and I fell about to Jeannete McDonald singing these words. The mystery of course was love and the sentiment the one marrying couples proclaim ... but just wait till decades down the track to see how the mystery unfolds. In the nursing home where my mother lives there is a man in his late '60s – he's been there a few years. Every day his wife comes to be with him, to sit with him in his room or on the verandah, to while away the day. Company for him, company for her. Surely other things in her life are left undone. Being with him is more important than all of that. She comes laden with food, clothes, activities. On the train. In 40 degree heat, through rain and icy wind.

This lady knows the mystery: how caring for another can enrich your life well beyond the excitement of finding "the one".

In the context of such a commitment, one poem in my collection reaches its full height. "The Promise of Marriage" is anonymous and presents a simple and realistic view of the hopes and reassurances that marriage may bring.

The poem's message is one of sharing through good times and bad, about having someone who will comfort, accept and support you no matter what.

71

About love

Robert Johnson is a psychologist who wrote much about love and respectful relationships in "Understanding the Psychology of Romantic Love" in 1983. While this excerpt doesn't soar with poetic splendour, it summarises the foundation for commitment and can be used in a wedding ceremony.

To me it is not just about romantic love but can apply to all kinds of love as an ideal basis for relationships.

If you want to talk about what love means to you, you could include this in your ceremony – it could be read at the beginning to set the tone:

> *Love is the power within us that affirms and values another human being as he or she is. Human love affirms that person who is actually there, rather than the ideal we would like him or her to be or the projection that flows from our minds. Love is the inner God who opens our blind eyes to the beauty, value, and quality of the other person. Love causes us to value that person as a total, individual self, and this means that we accept the negative side as well as the positive, the imperfections as well as the admirable qualities. When we truly love the human being rather than the projection, we love the shadow just as we love the rest. We accept the other person's totality.*
>
> *Human love causes us to see the intrinsic*

value of the person; therefore love leads us to honour and serve, rather than try to use the person for the purpose of ego. When love is guiding, we are concerned with the needs and well-being of the other, not fixated on our own wants and whims.

Love alters our sense of importance. Through love we see that the other individual has as great a value in the cosmos as our own; it becomes just as important to us that he or she should be whole, should live fully, should find the joy in life, as that our own needs be met.

Love leads towards the goodness, the value and the needs of the people around us. In its very essence, love is an appreciation, a recognition of another's value.

72

The commitment of love

Thomas à Kempis was a medieval Christian monk and a prolific writer. He wrote this about love, and the commitment of love. Of course the love he speaks about is not just romantic love but a code for living. How could an old guy in the Middle Ages write so fittingly of modern love?

Love is a great thing, a great good in every way; it alone lightens that which is heavy, and leads smoothly over all roughness. For it carries a burden without being burdened, and makes every bitter thing sweet and tasty. Love wants to be lifted up, not held back by anything low. Love wants to be free, and far from all worldly desires, so that its inner vision may not be dimmed nor good fortune bind it nor misfortune cast it down. Nothing is sweeter than love; nothing stronger, nothing higher, nothing wider; nothing happier, nothing fuller, nothing better in heaven and earth.

Love keeps watch and is never unaware, even when it sleeps; tired, it is never exhausted; hindered, it is never defeated; alarmed, it is never afraid; but like a living flame and a burning torch it bursts upward and blazes forth ...

Love is quick, sincere, dutiful, joyous and pleasant; brave, patient, faithful, prudent, serene and vigorous; and it never seeks itself.

For whenever we seek ourselves, we fall away from love. Love is watchful, humble and upright; not weak or frivolous, or directed toward vain things; temperate, pure, steady, calm, and alert in all the senses. Love is devoted and thankful, always trusting and hopeful, even when it doesn't taste the sweetness, for without pain, no-one can live in love.

73
Love and friendship

Some say that the basis for love in marriage is friendship. That friends turn into lovers and surely their relationship will grow and thrive. Laura Hendrick's poem "Love Is Friendship Caught Fire" suggests this and works nicely as the first reading in a wedding ceremony. In it, the poet talks about love which is founded on trust and acceptance, and the sharing of everyday ups and downs. A solid friendship. If you do not have it, nothing else will ever be enough, she writes.

I think that the love we hold as the essential ingredient to modern marriage surely doesn't begin with friendship. It doesn't ring true to me that you can be friends and not notice that you are attracted on quite a different level! What I do think though is that when the novelty and the excitement have died down and you find friendship – when your partner is the first person you turn to – then you have the essence of marriage. But your spouse will always be much more than a friend, and if you can keep the spark of lust and mutual interests that attracted you to one another in the first place alive, then you have a partnership that will stand up to time. You will maintain the passion, and it will be more than enough.

In her poem "The Perfect Love, the Perfect Friend" Reneé Duvall speaks first of passion, then of friendship. There is an intensity unique to passion that underpins the exclusivity of romantic love, the blindness of it. Then when this subsides and you find you also have support, understanding and unconditional devotion, you will have found the "perfect love, the perfect friend."

74
Special friends

The Prophet is a book by Lebanese-American poet and philosopher Kahlil Gibran who was born in 1883. The renown of *The Prophet* is still cult-like and excerpts are often quoted at weddings.

In pursuing the theory that the basis for a good marriage is friendship, it is worth looking at what Gibran wrote in "On Friendship". This poem is not about romantic love but it is about an intimate, enduring bond integral to marriage and platonic relationships equally. The distinction between casual friendships and the friendship which defines a real union is that the former is better described as "friendliness", general in nature; it is not a bond. But the friendship which evolves through marriage is a bond between souls – a bond in a good way (be advised of Gibran's best known poem, which tells us *not* to make a bond of love!).

Choosing excerpts of "On Friendship" would work at your wedding: to have the whole piece read is perhaps too philosophical – it is after all marriage that you're pinning down.

Here it is:

> *Your friend is your needs answered.*
> *He is your field which you sow with love and*
> *reap with thanksgiving.*
> *And he is your board and your fireside.*
> *For you come to him with your hunger, and*
> *you seek him for peace.*

*When your friend speaks his mind you fear
not the "nay" in your own mind, nor do you
withhold the "ay."*
*And when he is silent your heart ceases not
to listen to his heart;*
*For without words, in friendship, all
thoughts, all desires, all expectations are
born and shared, with joy that is
unacclaimed.*
*When you part from your friend, you grieve
not;*
*For that which you love most in him may be
clearer in his absence, as the mountain to
the climber is clearer from the plain.*
*And let there be no purpose in friendship
save the deepening of the spirit.*
*For love that seeks aught but the disclosure
of its own mystery is not love but a net cast
forth: and only the unprofitable is caught.*
And let your best be for your friend.
*If he must know the ebb of your tide, let him
know its flood also.*
*For what is your friend that you should seek
him with hours to kill?*
Seek him always with hours to live.
*For it is his to fill your need, but not your
emptiness.*
*And in the sweetness of friendship let there
be laughter, and sharing of pleasures.*
*For in the dew of little things the heart finds
its morning and is refreshed.*

75

I marry my friend

Friendship is definitely an ingredient in a good marriage. It is a simple and naïve view that it is the only ingredient, otherwise friends would be getting married as a matter of course. The person you marry is much more than a friend. However, the relationship sparked by the passion that insists on union evolves into many things – a "mate" I think is one of them, a partner in sharing the highs and lows of life, and in that sense, a friend. Hopefully, a best friend, distinguished from other friends in that you are mutually exclusive, unique to one another.

This short reading, whose author is unspecified, is one of the most popular choices in civil ceremonies and is just so right delivered around the time vows are exchanged. In one ceremony, the couple recited it to one another, alternating in reading a line, and then, together, the last line. It really adds a personal touch to do something like this in your ceremony. It is known as "Today".

> *Today I marry my friend;*
> *The one I have laughed with and cried with,*
> *The one I have learned from and shared*
> *with,*
> *The one I have chosen to support, encourage*
> *And give myself to*
> *Through all the days given us to share,*
> *Today I marry the one I love.*

And this charming piece from the Yueh-Fu genre of folk ballads, passed down during the Han Dynasty from 206 BC, makes this commitment:

> *I want to be your friend forever and ever.*
> *When the hills are all flat*
> *And the rivers are all dry,*
> *When the trees blossom in winter*
> *And the snow falls in summer,*
> *When heaven and earth mix –*
> *Not till then will I part from you.*

76
Building your relationship

It may seem the celebrant is imparting personal views about love and marriage but this should not be the case. Except for the legal words, the content of the ceremony is the choice of the couple, the expression of which is shared with guests through the facilitation of the celebrant.

Another reading about friendship being the firmest foundation for a lasting relationship is by Thomas Davidson, who died in 1900. It is called "Every Two Unique".

It describes this friendship as one which overtakes all other friendships. It is typified by a joining to achieve shared objectives while appreciating differences and unique qualities.

Love becomes friendship and friendship becomes love:

> *No human relationship gives one possession of another. A relationship links two people together. Each person is unique and different so the mode and style of this linking varies. But whether it is friendship or love, the two people side by side find and achieve so much together, which one of them cannot find or achieve alone.*
>
> *In a relationship the lover recognises the talent and beauty of the other. They should tell the other of it when they see it. In a*

relationship if you accept the sunshine and warmth, you must also be able to accept the overcast and the cool.

Among intelligent people, the surest basis of the relationship of marriage is friendship – the sharing of real interests – the ability to work through real issues together, to work towards common goals together, and to understand and share each other's thoughts and dreams.

77

Keeping your relationship healthy

I wonder if it's possible to offer a prescription for a sound relationship? And on whose evidence and experience? Here is something once suggested to me – 10 pointers. Should there be fewer? Why stop at 10?

- Be constant with communication, but be slow to criticise

- Accept fair criticism – take responsibility without being defensive

- Realise your behaviour has an effect on your partner and try to influence each other in respectful ways

- Compromise when you differ and respect your differences

- Speak freely – some conflict is normal, but show empathy

- Expect your partner to change and accept this growth

- Use less confrontational language – e.g. in tense moments use "I feel …", "I want …" to express your feelings rather than blaming your partner

- Don't presume to know what your partner is thinking or going to say

- Be assertive, not aggressive: keep your "power" equal

- Be quick to apologise when you are at fault

Sorted!

78
Being a good partner

I was reading about the disposability of marriage and the phases of true love. Enduring love happens at the Deep Love Phase, after the initial Romantic Phase and the negotiating of the Conflict Phase.

By this phase communicating and connecting skills have been learned and counter the option of disposing; they lead through to the final satisfying stage.

One of my clients sent me some similar research on Relationship Science by Samantha Joel, which describes these learned skills. It talks about the import of a wedding (or a commitment) ceremony which has two functions: to bring a private commitment into the public domain of recognition, and, significantly, to orient the relationship into the future. Hence, promises for an enduring partnership are fundamental to the ceremony.

To make this partnership happy and fulfilling as well, psychologists talk of 10 specific habits or behaviours:

- Focus on the positives and support your partner's independent goals

- Respect your partner's viewpoint and right to make individual choices

- Understand your partner's needs and strive to meet them

- Be prepared to make personal sacrifices to do this — not because you feel you "should" but because you want to make your partner happy

- Be the person in your partner's life they can most confidently rely on for support
- Always encourage your partner in their endeavours and make them feel good about themselves – give praise generously
- Do happy, interesting things together – keep your relationship out of a rut
- Face challenges together – act as a team, always keeping your partner's welfare and your relationship uppermost
- Give to your relationship willingly without thinking what you will get in return
- Never take each other for granted. Always tell your partner how much you love and appreciate them

The final point takes us full circle back to the first. And that is it, a good partnership is a circle of attraction, understanding, giving and growth. A wedding ring!

Chapter 10
Your Vows

79

You think you know what love is?

I take you to be my lawful wife, to have and to hold, from this day forward, for better, for worse, in good times and adversity, in sickness and in health, to love and cherish till death do us part ...

In the nursing home where my mother lives there is a married couple, Ron and Marion. Marion is in slightly better shape than Ron, but both live to varying degrees in that private, disconnected, isolating world of dementia. Physically, though, they are together – they share a room and their beds have been pushed together. I'm sure that their minds and spirits are still connected too and am absolutely certain their hearts are. They spend the day moving from one lounge area to another, sitting side by side to take their meals.

Another bed-ridden lady resident is visited every day by her husband. Sometimes he sits beside her while she wails incessantly, sometimes she is calm and they hold hands, sometimes she nods off and he keeps vigil with his head resting on the bed-head.

When I was leaving the other day an anxious assistant in nursing was urgently calling for assistance from the registered nurse – another devoted husband was trying to wheel his wife's care chair out the front door. It was physical, the struggle: the chair spinning in circles as he pulled it this way, the nurse the other.

"Let me through, I'm taking her home!" he cried in that thin, fragile aged voice. "She's coming home with me!!!" And all the time his frail, bewildered beloved weeping and trembling and pleading with him, "Oh let me stay, darling, please let me stay. Be a good boy and let me stay."

As long as we both shall live.

80

Variations on vows

The legal, binding vows of marriage are quite specific and cannot be altered. You must use each other's full names and say "I call upon the persons here present to witness that I take you as my lawful wife (or husband, spouse or partner in marriage, as appropriate)."

You can throw in the word "wedded" or use "everyone here" – but those are the only variants allowed.

However, you can also make your own personal vows to each other and in those you can use whatever words you like, as long as they don't negate the legal statement!

Here are some vows that maintain the ritual and beliefs of the pagan ceremonies I have described elsewhere :

> "We call upon all spirits and energies who serve the light, and you here present to witness how we two take the vows of marriage.
> By this fire which warms us both ..." *(pass hands through candle flame)*
> "... by this water which together we drink ..." *(celebrant offers goblet)*
> by the breath of our love which binds our hearts together,
> by these rings whose precious metal the earth provides,
> so we engage in solemn wedlock in accordance with the laws of man, the universal love of God, and the benevolent grace of nature."

I usually advise couples to make the personal vow first and then to seal it with the legal words. After these words have been exchanged, the marriage has taken place. That is a nice moment to savour before the public announcement or the signing of the documents (without which the marriage is still legal).

81

Your own vows

The vows you make on the wedding day are the essence of your marriage and the foundation of your relationship. Before you are married you should spend some time figuring out what it is you are promising to your partner. This is worth more than marriage education that can be imposed on you by others! Say what you mean on the day and mean what you say and you can't go wrong.

These personal vows were really nicely executed: sometimes couples will keep their vows from each other until the day of the wedding, but these vows were worked on by the couple together, alternating their well thought-out promises:

> "When I stand before you, I promise to guard and protect, and be the guide to direct you,"
> "When I stand before you, I promise to be inspirational and encouraging, yet patient and comforting;"
> "And when I stand behind you, I will encourage and motivate, and entrust my strength and discipline to you,"
> "And when I stand behind you I will be proud and trusting, and provide support that is both gracious and generous;"
> "And when I stand beside you, I will stimulate and challenge you, and explore and share with you,"
> "And when I stand beside you, I promise to be sharing and honest, genuine and loving;"

"Today it is with pride that I take you as my wife (or husband, spouse or partner, as appropriate)."

82

I cannot promise

This is one of the first variations on marriage vows that I came across – a couple I was marrying in the '90s came up with these promises:

> "Today as I take you for my wife (or husband,
> spouse or partner, as appropriate),
> I cannot promise you
> that I will not change or
> that my faults will never show.
> I cannot promise you
> that I will not have many different moods or
> never be erratic.
> I cannot promise you
> that I will not hurt your feelings sometimes
> or that I will always be strong.
> But I can promise you
> that I will always be supportive of you and
> understand everything that you do.
> I can promise you
> that I will share my thoughts and feelings
> with you and
> always laugh and cry with you.
> I can promise you
> that I will give you freedom to be yourself
> and help you achieve your goals.
> I can promise you
> that I will always be faithful to you and
> always be completely honest with you.
> And most of all,
> I can promise you that I will always love
> you."

These words have proved a very popular choice – they get a response from the wedding guests because they are realistic and personal. In fact there is great potential for personalising these vows further – you could use them as a model for describing individual traits. You are only limited by your literary ability and imagination.

83
Three commitments

These three versions of wedding vows are words of commitment befitting the pledge between any definition of the couple.

They are perfect as personal vows before the legal commitment is made:

> "You are my best friend, my partner and my true love,
> I will love you forever, and under all circumstances,
> I will stand by you always, in good times and bad,
> I will have faith in you and encourage you in everything that you do,
> I will listen to you, laugh with you, and hold you,
> I will work with you as we build our lives together,
> I will be your best friend, your partner and your true love,
> Till death do us part."

And this:

> "From the beginning, I knew you were meant for me. The oceans could not keep us apart; and today, as you become my lawful wife (or husband, spouse or partner, as appropriate) in marriage, all is as it should be. I accept you not only as my friend and lover, but also as my teacher and my guide, through the seasons of

our new life in marriage.

I will laugh with you in the joys and happiness of the summertimes: I will offer you patience and understanding through the changes of the autumns; I will give you support and tenderness when you most need them in the winters; I will share with you the new beginnings and possibilities of the springtimes. But above all I will love and honour you as my wife, husband, spouse, partner (as appropriate) till the end of our days. These are my vows to you."

And this:

"I take you as my wife (or husband, spouse or partner, as appropriate) in marriage, beside me and apart from me, in laughter and in tears, in conflict and in serenity, asking that you be no other than yourself, loving what I know of you, trusting what I do not yet know, in all the ways that life may lead us."

84

I commit myself

Walter Rinder is an American humanist writer who was born in the '30s but was most prolific in the '70s … one of his famous works was published in 1984 as an essay called "The Spectrum of Love". His writings are an exploration of the concept of love and of the commitment that underpins love of all kinds really. He is gay and that is neither here nor there, except to demonstrate that love transcends gender, colour and creed.

In the excerpt in my material, "I commit myself …" Walter Rinder talks of a sincere interest in the other's sense of self and happiness and of the need to present himself as authentically as possible. He says that love has opened up possibilities of universal connectedness and kindness.

It fits beautifully with the ten ways of being a good partner I described earlier. You could use them with this reading to come up with your bespoke version of commitment.

You could use this before the legal vows are exchanged.

85

Promises, promises

These anonymous promises don't compare with the great poets for heart-stopping impact, but they do sum up sentiments that may just perfectly reflect what you are pledging to commit.

You could have the celebrant read them on your behalf before you exchange the legal vows, or you could read them to each other, maybe taking a promise each, as they are quite long … remember your guests will be hearing them twice otherwise.

While the ceremony is for you, you don't want people tuning out. So I wouldn't use these as your personal vows repeated after the celebrant, leading to people hearing them four times. Therefore, losing impact. It's an accessible reading though and can be nicely integrated into your legal vows.

> "I promise to give you the best of myself
> and to ask of you no more than you can give.
> I promise to respect you as your own person
> and to realise that your interests, desires and needs
> are no less important than my own.
> I promise to share with you my time and my attention
> and to bring joy, strength and imagination to our relationship.
> I promise to keep myself open to you
> and to let you see through the window of my world into my innermost fears and feelings,

secrets and dreams.
I promise to grow along with you
and to be willing to face changes in order to
keep our relationship alive and exciting.
I promise to love you in good times and in
bad
with all l have to give and all I feel inside
in the only way I know how.
Completely and forever."

Actually you could play around and personalise these promises – use them as a model and make your alterations so that they say all you want to say.

86
The promise of safety

In a world of uncertainty people seek a sense security where they can – in their jobs, their families and in their personal relationships. Wedding promises are the foundation for safety into the future: your marriage will be the one thing that you can count on, to all intents and purposes your commitment will remain unaltered, even if your circumstances don't.

If you want to express this in a poem, "I will be here" by Steven Curtis Chapman is perfect.

The poet describes how he will support his partner when life seems threatening and unpredictable and when doubt and the ravages of time set in. This poem would be just right before you exchange the legal commitment; it could be your "personal vow" and could be read by you to each other – a stanza each and then the last together, your voices blending, why not? There would be emotion in that. Your ceremony does not have to be a flawless piece of theatre – tears and laughter and stumbling are what make it you.

87

Ten promises

According to law in Australia these are the words that make a marriage:

> "I call upon the persons here present to witness that I take you as my lawful wedded wife (or husband, spouse or partner in marriage, as appropriate)".

Referred to as *The Vows*, they are really a binding statement of intent, and in that sense a commitment.

But what really makes the marriage in the hearts of the couple are their personal promises, the bespoke and thoughtful vows for the future.

Here are ten promises you can make based on Samantha Joel's ways to be a good partner:

- to understand wishes, fears and dreams
- to support ambitions and share in achievements and disappointments
- to respect identity and opportunities for growth
- to be constant and help overcome challenges
- to recognise the right to individual choices
- to do what is in your partner's best interests
- to maintain compassion above "fairness"
- to keep life exciting, fun and passionate
- to show appreciation every day
- to always be there when your partner needs you

These promises are absolute and a wonderful base to mindfulness in a relationship – you can use them and modify them to represent the reality you can expect in your own commitment. Enjoy writing your own version!

Chapter 11
Words from the Heart

88
Intimate poems

There are poems so intimate that sharing them publicly is almost intrusive. These poems celebrate the moment of love found. They relinquish a loveless and unfulfilled past and brim with wonder and hope for the future. They speak of time standing still: past, present and future are all caught up in the moment of "I do".

Judith Wright wrote such a poem, "In Praise of Marriages", first published in 1953:

Not till life halved, and parted
one from the other,
did time begin, and knowledge,
sorrow, delight.
Terror of being apart, being lost,
made real the night.
Seeking and finding made
yesterday, now and tomorrow;
and love was realised first
when those two came together.

So perilously joined,
lighted in one small room,
we have made all things true.
Out of the you and I
spreads this field of power,
that all that waits may come,
all possibles be known —

> *all futures step their stone*
> *and parts come into flower.*

This moment is captured in an excerpt from Sharon Old's poem, "The Wedding Vow":

> *… we stood*
> *holding each other by the hand …*
> *… I felt as if I had come*
> *to claim a promise …*
> *I felt as if*
> *I had come, congenitally unworthy, to beg.*
> *And yet, I had been working toward this love*
> *all my life. And then it was time*
> *to speak — he was offering me, no matter*
> *what, his life. That is all I had to*
> *do there, to accept that gift*
> *I had longed for — to say I had accepted it,*
> *as if being asked if I breathe. Do I take?*
> *I do. I take as he takes — we have been practising this.*
> *Do you bear this pleasure? I do.*

89
Change of status

The exchange of marriage vows instantly changes your status from separate to conjoined – a fact that is realised in your hearts long before this moment. The pledges made publicly are just the formal marking of inner peace and fulfilment. The pledges that you make to each other are that you will do all you can to prevent the power of this moment from changing.

Recently a couple I married wanted me to elicit these three commitments from them as they stood before their witnesses, together:

> "Do you pledge to help each other to develop your hearts and minds, cultivating compassion, generosity, concentration, patience, enthusiasm and wisdom as you age and undergo the various ups and downs of life and to transform them into the path of love, joy and equanimity?"
>
> "Do you pledge to preserve and enrich your affection for each other? To take the loving feelings you have for one another and your vision for each other's potential and inner beauty and to radiate this love outwards?"
>
> "Do you pledge continuously to strive to remember your own Being, as well as the true nature of all living things? To maintain the awareness that all things are temporary, and to remain optimistic so that you can achieve your greatest potential and lasting happiness?"

This excerpt from Edith Aynsley's poem "Marriage Lines" follows well from these questions:

I love and respect you, not only for what you are to me,
not only for what you will give to me, but for what you will give
to Humanity.

The world is our home,
Humankind our family.

We shall possess not each other,
For possession is destruction.

I promise you only to be myself and to help you to be yourself.
To reach our real selves we must grow, develop, change.

I pray I may never use you to inflate my own ego
but encourage you to nurture all that is best in you
for the sake of Humanity.

90

What you are to me

And what makes your partner worthy of love? Far from personal charm it is how you are transformed by love that makes you love in return. True, requited love gives and gives, as Roy Croft writes in this excerpt from his poem "Love":

I love you,
Not only for what you are,
But for what I am
When I am with you.

I love you,
Not only for what
You have made of yourself,
But for what
You are making of me.

I love you
For the part of me
That you bring out;
I love you
For putting your hand
Into my heaped-up heart
And passing over
All the foolish, weak things
That you can't help
Dimly seeing there,
And for drawing out

Into the light
All the beautiful belongings
That no one else had looked
Quite far enough to find.

I love you
Because you have done
More than any creed
Could have done
To make me good,
And more than any fate
To make me happy.

You have done it
Without a touch,
Without a word,
Without a sign.
You have done it
By being yourself.

91
The promise of refuge

The idea that in finding a loving partner we are finding a place of refuge underlies the trust peculiar to marriage and commitment. The union of two is exclusive, private and special, a place where you can breathe and rest and be yourself. This might be something you want to acknowledge in your ceremony. Many poems talk of this.

These two are intimate poems of commitment which you could read to each other.

The first is called "Love-Amored" and was written last century by MaryLu Terral Jeans. They bear the same message:

> *My love surrounds the house in which you dwell,*
> *The place your work, the streets your feet have known,*
> *With more of tenderness than I can tell,*
> *And prayers I have said for you alone.*
> *If you are lonely, know that I am near;*
> *If you are sad, my faith will comfort you,*
> *The things you value I shall hold most dear;*
> *Your happiness will make me happy, too.*
> *Be sure of this: Though you may travel far,*
> *My love will guard you anywhere you are.*

The second is anonymous:

> *There is a place within my heart*
> *Where memories of you lie.*

A place I visit from time to time;
A place that will never die.
A place that no-one knows about
Except for a very few.
A place that I have set aside
Especially for you.

I go to this place whenever I feel
Lonely when we're apart.
I go to this place whenever I need
You to touch my heart .
You shall always be in this place,
For I give my heart to you.

If not these, why not find a poem that sums up your feelings and present it as a gift to your beloved on your wedding day? A poem each.

92

Why marriage?

Meeting someone with whom you are willing to share your life is for many a dream come true. In fact, when you've met that person, being apart is unthinkable. But the prospect of finding your perfect match isn't just something that makes your heart flutter … the happiness is founded in the certainty that here is someone who complements you and makes you feel better, more secure, more content than when you were single.

Here is how Susan Polis Schutz describes this transition:

When I was younger I dreamed how a relationship should be
a sharing of goals and lives
A love so strong that it is always exciting and growing
A blending of two imperfect individuals into stronger, better
people
who laugh more, are happier, more successful
and more at peace.
My dream came to be because you had the same dream as I
And I want you to know how thankful I am
For our beautiful relationship and how much I love you.

"Why Marriage" is the title of a poem by contemporary American poet Mari Nichols.

It would be beautifully placed at the beginning of the ceremony – maybe after the introduction and welcome to guests. It is a personal view on what the commitment to marriage means. The reading talks of a certain integrity, a quality which the bond of marriage brings. This union is about being with someone who knows you through and through and whose life is made better because of you; it is a platform for growth and individual endeavours. The poem is a tribute to mutual respect and a commitment to taking responsibility in partnership. It was published in the 1980s and is amongst my collection since being brought to me by a couple recently.

Marriage alone doesn't create this quality: the relationship does that, but having reached it, marriage is a logical conclusion.

93
Transforming love

The experience of love, when it hits you that you have found "the one", can change your life in an instant. "What a difference a day makes" says the song – and it's true: it is the feeling that gets you first; it is certainly the heart, not the head, processing this. Everything is brighter, richer, fuller when you are buzzing along with (especially new-found) love. Clearing rain is a metaphor often used for re-birth, a clean canvas for the emergence of emotions and possibilities … this simple anonymous poem captures this wonder – called "Renewal":

> *The rain had ceased to fall,*
> *new light gave new colour*
> *to leaves and songs of birds.*
>
> *You quietly entered the room,*
> *softly your arms entwined me*
>
> *And sunshine followed rain,*
> *new love gave new colour*
> *to leaves and songs of birds.*

In his "A Marriage", Mark Twain uses a mathematical metaphor for the enrichment of union:

> *A marriage …*
> *makes of two fractional lives*
> *a whole,*
> *it gives to two purposeless lives*

a work, and doubles the strength
of each to perform it,
it gives to two
questioning natures
a reason for living,
and something to live for,
it will give a new gladness
to the sunshine,
a new fragrance to the flowers,
a new beauty to the earth,
and a new mystery to life.

I could imagine the first poem read at the beginning of the ceremony, and Mark Twain's right at the end – the first about the power of the beloved to transform, the second about the evolution of the relationship to marriage and its potential.

94
The final word

There are hundreds and hundreds of poems and formal words of wisdom that could be read at wedding ceremonies. I've chosen just a few that have proven to be popular over the years, and some which are my favourites that I wish people would choose.

This one is a personal gift from one lover to another; it could close the ceremony and be read by them, not me.

It's by the American poet, e.e. cummings, who was prolific in the first half of the 20th century and died in 1962. His unconventional punctuation contributes significantly to the idea of the dreamy, pervasive power of love to infiltrate the depths of your soul, a power driven by itself and out of your control. As Sir Philip Sidney writes in "The Bargain", cummings talks of the "just exchange" of hearts, in which "my true love hath my heart, and I have his":

> *I carry your heart with me (I carry it in*
> *my heart) I am never without it (anywhere*
> *i go you go, my dear; and whatever is done*
> *by only me is your doing, my darling)*
>
> *i fear*
>
> *no fate (for you are my fate, my sweet) i want*
> *no world (for beautiful you are my world, my true)*

and it's you whatever a moon has always meant
and whatever a sun will always sing is you

here is the deepest secret nobody knows
(here is the root of the root and the bud of the bud
and the sky of the sky of a tree called life; which grows
higher than the soul can hope or mind can hide)
and this is the wonder that's keeping the stars apart

i carry your heart (I carry it in my heart)

The poem talks about peace, security, strength, trust and comfort – it says it all.

Chapter 12
Blessings on your Marriage

95
Word of the day

Here's rather an ugly word for an occasion otherwise characterised by beauty: *epithalamium*. It is from the Greek, "epithalamios", meaning nuptials, and is a poem or a song in honour of the bride and groom. Originally it was sung by children to a bride and groom at the door of the bridal chamber on their wedding night. Weddings have been the inspiration for poetry since ancient times when blessings were evoked and often allusions made to nymphs, gods and goddesses. It was first used in literature by Sappho.

> *Raise up the roof tree —*
> *a wedding song!*
> *High up carpenters —*
> *A wedding song!*
> *The bridegroom is coming,*
> *The equal of Ares,*
> *much bigger than a big man.*

Ares is the Greek god of war, the son of Zeus and Hera and one of the most powerful gods on Mt Olympus. Ares married Aphrodite; they had eight children, one of whom was Eros, the god of love.

By the way, Sappho died in 560 BC. She wrote about love and physical bewitchment. She wrote about men. And she wrote about women.

In relationships, there is nothing new under the sun. Nothing.

96
A modern epithalamium

Although these poems originated in Roman times they enjoyed a revival in the Renaissance in the work of Spenser, John Donne, Ben Johnson … one of the finest was the 23 stanzas Spenser wrote about each hour of his own wedding day.

If you are looking for an anthology of poetry and prose written for weddings, including the above, you should look at Robert Hass' and Stephen Mitchell's classic collection, "Into the Garden – A Wedding Anthology".

However there are modern epithalamia too – the poems that are read aloud in wedding ceremonies are just this. They are universally delivered to celebrate the joy of union, bestow felicitations on the couple and invoke blessings and best wishes for future harmony and happiness in marriage. There are hundreds on the internet – some of them original compositions for particular ceremonies. You could ask someone to write one for you!

97
Simple blessings

Some blessings are not overly laden with philosophy but in their simplicity they appeal to the universe, like the original epithalamia, to look after the newly-weds as they embark on their new journey through the seasons and twists and turns of life.

Both suggest that the couples have faith in the universe to protect and keep their love.

This one is anonymous. You can see how you might have a special blessing written for you based on something like this.

> *The wonderful joys that the future will hold will be found in the plans that you make, the roads that you travel, the sights that you see and the paths that you let your hearts take.*
> *So believe in your dreams, in your hopes and your goals and the trust that you place in each other.*
> *And know that, wherever love leads you, you'll go step by step and beside one another.*
> *We wish you a beautiful life journey together – beginning with this special day of happiness and love.*

Another popular blessing I can show you was written by a South Australian author called Nan Whitcomb who trained as a nurse and air hostess in the 1950s. In the 1970s she published three volumes of simple poetry entitled "The Thoughts of Nanushka". One of her poems, "To Mourn Too Long For Those We Love", was read at the funeral of Michael Hutchence.

Her wedding blessing, "May your friendship and trust …" talks about the growth of your married life through passing seasons, of renewal and strength, until the seasons become a lifetime spent together.

98
The gift of a blessing

So a wedding is not only the declaration of a union but the opportunity for the invited to have their say – to cast a bespoke or borrowed blessing on the newly-weds (coming as it should after the binding is made). The blessing is the finishing touch to the ceremony – the gift from all present, far more important than the dinner sets and wine glasses. There is an infinite number of blessings – a blessing for every couple from here to eternity. And blessings are timeless.

James Dillet Freeman was an American minister of the Unity Church. Of Cherokee and English/Irish descent, Freeman identified with Native American culture and was a prolific poet who explored the human condition, not only in his writing, but as a speaker. He wrote of love and loss, longing and fulfilment, tragedy and contentment. Although it has been read at countless weddings, his "Blessing for a Marriage" is so personal that it seems it was especially written for every couple who hears it:

> *May your marriage bring you all the exquisite excitements a marriage should bring, and may life grant you also patience, tolerance and understanding. May you need one another, but not out of weakness. May you want one another, but not out of lack. May you entice one another, but not compel one another. May you embrace one another,*

but not encircle one another. May you succeed in all-important ways with one another, and not fail in the little graces. May you look for things to praise, often say "I love you!" and take no notice of small faults.

If you have quarrels that push you apart, may both of you hope to have good sense enough to take the first step back. May you enter into the mystery that is the awareness of one another's presence – no more whimsical than spiritual, warm and near when you are side by side, and warm and near when you are in separate rooms or distant cities.

May you have happiness, and may you find it in making one another happy. May you have love, and may you find it in loving one another.

99
Is it as simple as this?

This is a blessing I'm often asked to include in a wedding ceremony.

Its simplicity and naiveté make it appeal to couples who find neither modern nor classical poetry suitable for their wedding; its hint of spiritualty substitutes warmly for religious invocations.

Although it is passed off as an authentic tribute to Apache culture, this reading first appeared in the 1947 novel by Elliot Arnold called "Blood Brothers" – which was later turned into the movie, "Broken Arrow". In the story the hero befriends the Indian chief, Cochise, and meets and marries the young woman, Morning Star. The poem was an invention of the author and has undergone many mutations, such is its popularity. To call it Apache is cultural appropriation I suppose, but only for the most benign reason. Such inventions and reflections are better known as "fakelore" than tradition, but they serve their purpose – here is one version:

> *Now you will feel no rain, for each of you will be the shelter to the other. Now you will feel no cold, for each of you will be warmth for the other. Now you are two persons, but there is only one life before you. Go now to your dwelling place to enter into the days of your life together. And may your days be good and long upon the earth. Treat yourselves and each other with respect, and remind*

yourselves often of what brought you together. Give the highest priority to the tenderness, gentleness and kindness that your connection deserves. When frustration, difficulty and fear assail your relationship – as they threaten all relationships at one time or another – remember to focus on what is right between you, not only the part which seems wrong. In this way, you can ride out the storms when clouds hide the face of the sun in your lives – remembering that even if you lose sight of it for a moment, the sun is still there. And if each of you takes responsibility for the quality of your life together, it will be marked by abundance and delight.

100
Good luck!

This anonymous reading is often used as a final blessing ... the fact that it suggests that the success of your marriage should be based on gentle manipulation is beside the point I suppose! It's humorous and realistic and talks of the balancing act that it sometimes takes to keep a relationship humming along.

When you marry her, love her.
After you marry her, study her.
When she is blue, cheer her.
When she is talkative, by all means, talk to her.
If she dresses well, compliment her.
When she is cross, humor her.
If she is jealous, cure her.
If she is lonely, comfort her.
When she looks pretty, tell her so.
Let her feel you understand her.
But never let her know she isn't boss.

When you marry him, love him.
After you marry him, study him.
If he is secretive, trust him.
If he is sad, cheer him.
When he is talkative, listen to him.
When he is quarrelsome, ignore him.
If he is jealous, cure him.
If he cares naught for pleasure, coax him.

If he favours society, accompany him.
When he deserves it, kiss him.
Let him think you understand him.
But never let him know you manage him.

Usually a family member will read this – an aunt, for example, in a position to offer such sage advice!

About the Author

In 1993, Susan decided she wanted to frock-up, recite poetry and help couples create a 30-minute masterpiece, "true to their relationship".

In July 1995, under the auspices of the Commonwealth Attorney General, she became an authorised marriage celebrant.

Now Susan has conducted over 1,000 ceremonies and wants to share her thoughts and ideas from a career dedicated to making lovers happy.

For more information, please visit:
ceremonybydesign.com.au

Photo by Jeff Davies